DRAMA AS A SECOND LANGUAGE
A practical handbook for language teachers
by
Suzanne Karbowska Hayes

ISBN 0 86082 430 6
Published by the National Extension College Trust Ltd.,
18 Brooklands Avenue, Cambridge CB2 2HN
Printed by NEC Print

Author: Suzanne Karbowska Hayes
Hammersmith and North Kensington Adult Education Institute
Designer: Vicky Squires

Contents

Acknowledgements

Many of the ideas in the book were generated in my classes at the Hammersmith and North Kensington Adult Education Institute and so thanks must go to the many students who participated so enthusiastically in the experimental work that led to the writing of this book.

Thanks also to Meryl Wilkins, a colleague and ESL teacher who read the book and offered some useful criticism and advice, and to Elizabeth Bartlett, another colleague and drama teacher with whom I worked closely and who provided many ideas, particularly in the movement section of the book.

I am grateful too to the many colleagues in the Inner London Education Authority who gave me encouragement and support in proceeding with this project.

Thanks also to Jullie Scarr for her contribution of the play *Shoplifter*.

Notes to readers

Throughout the book I have used the feminine pronoun as a linguistic convenience to avoid the clumsiness of she/he and his/hers, etc.

My aim is to make the material in this book accessible to a wide range of language and adult basic education teachers. I have therefore tried to explain all the teaching terms used in the book, although I realise at times that my explanations may appear too simplistic for specialist teachers.

Preface

The purpose of this book is to share with language teachers my ideas and experience of teaching drama and to offer some practical suggestions and advice on setting up a drama class for language students or introducing drama into existing language learning classes.[1]

Non-drama specialists may feel a little apprehensive about using this new approach, but they should not be deterred from employing the techniques of drama in their classes as they should find that, as experienced language teachers, they already possess many of the skills needed in initiating and presenting these activities. It is hoped that the book will provide constructive guidelines which will allay fears, activate teachers' own imaginations and give them the confidence to invent and devise other activities specifically related to their own students' needs.

This is not an academic book but one based almost entirely on personal experience. Most of the ideas presented here are the result of work done with two distinct groups of students over a period of three years. The first groups were made up of post-elementary second language learners from a variety of ethnic backgrounds who were attending language classes at an adult education centre: the second groups comprised adult native speakers, some of whom had literacy problems and/or difficulty in expressing themselves effectively. For each group a special two-hour drama class was established, which met once a week and was described in our publicity as a class designed both to help students gain confidence, fluency and self-expression and to improve communication skills through drama. Students were offered the drama class as an extra option which they could attend in addition to their normal language classes. To many people the idea of doing drama would be anathema, so when trying to establish a new drama class a certain amount of encouragement and persuasion may be called for. My own policy is to explain to students what I hope they will achieve through drama and to invite them to come along and try the class out. For some students one visit may be enough, but the majority of students respond well and look forward to their class, once they have overcome any initial shyness and apprehension.

If it is organisationally practical to set up a special drama class rather than try to incorporate bits of drama into an ordinary language class, I think it is preferable for the following reasons. Students have enrolled voluntarily for drama and, whilst they may not know exactly what it is, they will be more open to drama techniques and leaving the teacher free from the need to worry about grammer, literacy, etc. which will be taken care of in other classes. Of course, drama techniques may be used in language classes to enhance their language learning and they may also be

---

1. By drama I mean using mime and movement, games, role-play and improvisation to develop language and social skills.

1

used to diagnose needs, but students who have come to a class expecting book-learning may not see the relevance of drama for them and may be hostile to the approach. If it is not possible to have a special drama class then I would suggest a regular drama slot in a class which meets often would be the next best thing.

It is my view that the general aims of using drama, which I shall describe later, apply to ESL and native speakers and most of the activities set out in the book have been found to be appropriate for use with both types of student. Some are specifically aimed at second language learners and these and the suitability of activities for various levels will be indicated. Although I have been working mainly with ESL students I would consider that the ideas contained in this book would also be suitable for EFL students and could even be adapted for use with native speakers studying a foreign language where a more active context is sought.

Learning through drama can be a rewarding and stimulating experience for both students and teachers and it is hoped that this book will provide a basis for experimentation and discovery in the classroom and encourage organisers to set up drama groups in their own establishments.

S.K.H.

1
Introduction

Language

Before suggesting a theoretical basis for using drama with students learning English let us first consider the language we are teaching, its function and the methods we employ.

Language is surely the most interesting, distinctive and important of all human activities. It enables us to have control over our environment and to determine how we live. We may think of it, perhaps, as having many of the characteristics of a code which has been agreed between peoples for the purpose of communication. Language enables us to communicate our needs within the community and to negotiate with others but it also most importantly allows us to express our own personality and uniqueness and to develop consciousness. The way in which we learn our native language involves the total personality and is therefore a creative process, but the way in which a second language is acquired is often mechanistic and artificial, depending on a theory of teaching which ignores the emotional and non-verbal content of language.[2]

In recent years there have been many innovations in language teaching and most teachers do not now teach structure and vocabulary in a vacuum but try to place language into a living context which is relevant to their students needs. The student who has reached the dizzy heights of mastering the third conditional, for example, and can now say: 'If I had won the football pools I would have bought a car' would not be considered proficient in the language unless he had also mastered its many functions. Teachers of ESL have recognised that the structural approach to language teaching is not by itself effective in developing communication skills which enable the learner to cope in everyday life situations and it certainly does not take account of the individuality of the learner. Ever since its early days in home tuition teachers have adopted a functional approach to language teaching which concentrates on providing students with the language skills needed to be effective and to be autonomous.[3]

Students come from a diversity of social, cultural and educational backgrounds, and their language level is not the only factor which determines their effective communication and control over their environment. Giving students confidence is a vital factor and this

---

2. By using a structural approach to language teaching I mean teaching the grammar of the language through a series of carefully graded sentence patterns from the simple tenses through to the more complex. The problem with this method is that form comes before meaning and the language learned, though grammatically correct, may not be appropriate to the students' needs.

3. By learning functions the student learns the patterns of behaviour that lie behind the language. They learn how to make requests, give information, express feelings and attitudes, agree, accept, persuade etc., and at all times the language is made relevant to their immediate needs of communication.

confidence can only come when they are able to express their own personality through the language.

Giving confidence is also the key to improved linguistic competence when teaching English to native speakers attending basic education courses. Apart from literacy problems, the ability to express themselves effectively and increase their word power depends to a large extent on confidence and developing self-esteem.

How do you teach confidence? It is my belief that it can be achieved by placing learning into an active context. It is gained by doing and speaking in front of other people; learning to think on one's feet; taking risks; trusting one's own judgement and finding resources in difficult situations. Language and confidence develop out of first-hand experience. The methods employed by most language teachers today help to develop the learner's confidence to use language effectively and to move from passive learning to active. But for imaginative and creative use of language one may turn to drama.

What is drama?

Education is concerned with individuals; drama is concerned with the individuality of individuals, with the uniqueness of each human essence.

Brian Way

Any attempt to define drama is an almost impossible task. Drama is somewhat intangible. Is it a subject? Is it a teaching method? Is it a process like movement is to dance? Is it an art form? Is it therapy?

The term 'drama' thus has a wide application and it can perhaps be best defined for our purposes by stating some educational aims. We are considering drama in education and specifically drama in language teaching so what exactly do we want to achieve?

First, through drama one can aim to increase the students self-esteem and self-presentation by using a teaching method which emphasises achievement and puts little stress on the 'right' or the 'wrong' way of doing things.

Secondly, one aims to increase self-confidence by providing students with direct experiences from which they can discover and develop their own strengths. Students can test the effectiveness of their use of language through drama, and increased competence through practise will increase confidence. For example, one doesn't improve one's interview technique by talking, one improves by doing, by making mistakes and correcting them.

Thirdly, one aims to improve the students' social awareness and interaction. Through drama students gain practice in relating to other individuals, to small groups and the whole group. They learn to give and take in a 'working' situation. They learn to use their initiative and to

5

develop sensitivity by working in pairs, and in improvisation in small or large groups.

Fourthly, one aims to improve a range of skills related to language learning. These are: *thinking,* by working out resolutions to problems in drama; *memory,* via games and exercises, designed to train the memory; *imagination,* through movement work and dramatic improvisation; *observation,* trained through games and sense-exercises extended in drama work and also *listening; verbal fluency,* developed through voice exercises, language games, role-play and improvisation; *extending ability to express emotional range,* important for personal development and links with increased verbal accuracy and fluency; *sense of form,* by developing a feeling for the need for preparation, climax, and resolution in all types of work.

Fifthly, one aims to increase the students awareness of the non-verbal elements of language and how to interpret and respond to them.[4]

Finally, the long-term aim of drama is simply to help students understand themselves and the world they live in and to gain insight into all kinds of human behaviour.

---

4. For the ESL student drama may help her improve her pronunciation, stress and intonation and all skills related to speaking.

2
A theoretical basis for using drama with ESL students and the role of the teacher

It is a fact that most ESL teachers use many of the techniques of drama in their everyday teaching, especially in the initial stages of learning, as a way of conveying meaning. Mime, gesture and acting-out are essential methods of communication with beginners and elementary students and it would be difficult to communicate without them. Through the para-language the meaning is made clear and unambiguous and the visual experience helps to fix the new language in the student's mind. To communicate the teacher must always be a creative actor but there is no reason why the students should remain a passive audience. From the early stages of language learning they can be encouraged to participate in the drama approach. Simple conversational exchanges and transactions assume more meaning if they are set in an active context, and many teachers do simulate real-life situations in the classroom through the use of role-play and improvisation. We remember things we experience far better than things we just think or read about. Role-play can be and often is a feature of the lesson throughout the learning process but at the more advanced stages it can be used in a variety of creative and interesting ways. (See the section on role-play and improvisation, chaps. 7 and 8).

Post-elementary students who have a good foundation of language experience are able to negotiate meaning in most everyday situations, but often lack an ability to express feelings, attitudes, and shades of meaning. They may find it difficult to interpret the social and cultural context, to understand behaviour and do not always have a flexible approach to their use of spoken language or an awareness of how other people respond to them and the nature of the response. Misunderstanding often arises because they do not always know that 'how, where and when' language is used determines the meaning.

Through drama the student learns to perceive and identify different situations, to assume an appropriate role, to understand different functions and points of view and to manipulate language accordingly. This is fundamental to the process of orientation in the new culture and to achieving autonomy within it.

In the drama lesson students talk more than before and exchanges are more spontaneous. They participate in their own learning process and gain confidence from the sense of security offered by the group. Everyone has a contribution to make and students who are weak linguistically often reveal unsuspected abilities. I had one student who, because of a speech impediment, was almost unintelligible, but he turned out to be such a superb mimic and master of facial expressions that his status in the group increased rapidly. Stronger students find themselves sharing their knowledge and shy students grow bolder. One student who was initially very inhibited and reluctant to perform complained towards the end of the first term that the part he was given in a play we were making was 'too small!' Sometimes a student who is shy in the classroom may blossom when protected by a role and reveal hidden depths.

Through drama situational English can be explored in total context. The text book may give us only the physical setting and the appropriate situational vocabulary and structural phrases. There are other elements which are equally important. The student needs to go behind the words to examine the functions, behaviour and feelings involved in the situation.

In life, roles are constantly changing: we are, in turn, passenger, customer, colleague, friend, husband/wife, teacher, etc., and the way we play these roles and the language we use is coloured by our status, self-image, moods, attitudes and feelings. If roles and personality are ignored we teach language in a vacuum. In any transaction, interaction or relationship the effect of what we say depends not only on the words we use but how we use them, and ESL learners need to learn how to use language appropriately. By subtle alterations of tone and emphasis we can modify or change the meaning of the words and structures we use. The same arrangement of words can be made polite, aggressive, tentative or pleading by changes of tonal quality, timing, stress and intonation and the accompanying facial expressions and body language. Drama techniques can directly engage the learner's feelings and make him aware that meaning is not conveyed just through words alone.[5]

Linguistic factors

Through drama the student is given the chance to take risks in the language, to try out new ways of combining words and phrases and to find out where there are gaps in her knowledge. Since drama uses what the students bring from their own experience it can help the teacher to diagnose what they already know and find out their level of language development.

It is possible to set up drama which will provide students with many language experiences which would not ordinarily be available and thereby to increase their linguistic competence and range. Through drama students may express, needs, feelings, attitudes and opinions. They may argue, persuade, justify, defend, complain, inform, instruct, report, explain, negotiate and mediate. They learn to link language to other forms of communication, that is gesture, facial expressions, body language and they increase their fluency.

Psychological factors

With limited or no knowledge of English the newcomer who is trying to establish herself in a new country and cultural environment may suffer severe depression and what may amount to a crisis of identity. We have all

---

5.   Through role-play the student can discover what it feels like to be on both sides of the exchange which can be a very revealing experience.

seen students who seem to be in a state of emotional paralysis. Opportunities for self-expression are severely limited. Without language one feels stupid, impotent and insignificant. The normal language class may give the student some scope to express her own personality and individuality and most ESL teachers treat their students as individuals and are concerned about their welfare, but through drama the student may really blossom. She has a chance to think and to act creatively and to assert her own personality and thus boost her confidence. As previously suggested, it is often the student who is weak linguistically who can dominate the drama class by bringing to it humour, sensitivity, imagination and gifts of mimicry. For the student suffering from stress and insecurity drama can be very therapeutic. I have known several students who were deeply troubled about their situation after fleeing from inhospitable political regimes who have found refuge and consolation in the drama class. Learning through drama is essentially fun and entering the world of make-believe allows us to push problems into the background for a while and return to the real world feeling refreshed. It can be extremely liberating to step outside oneself and enter the realms of the imagination to become another personality.

Cultural factors

Students come from many widely differing cultural backgrounds. Through drama, cultural differences are spontaneously revealed and by examining these differences students can begin to understand each other and gain insight into the way the British behave, which may seem to be peculiar at times. Prejudice is based on ignorance and it is not enough to teach language. One must also teach the cultural context in which this language is used. This is not to suggest that we expect students to adopt our culture, but simply to understand the cultural environment in which they find themselves and its implications for them. In the drama class the student will discover that the way to approach a situation in this country is often very different from how it would be in their own. They may choose to reject our ways, but at least they should be aware of them.

Drama involves students working together very closely and intimately. Co-operation, communication and mutual support are essential and through these close relationships cultural and racial barriers are broken down. If a Moroccan girl, for example, plays the role of the wife of a Vietnamese boy in an improvisation, the experience will bring them closer. I am not suggesting that any romantic liaisons have developed between students in my drama classes but certainly friendships are inevitable. Drama involves the exposure of attitudes and opinions in spontaneous response through acting. In effect this means revealing oneself – offering and building on each other's contributions as a way of developing understanding both of each other and of issues at hand.[6]

Social factors

Drama is essentially social interaction. Acting out can help students experiment with the appropriateness of a number of social registers and help to build up a more flexible approach to life and other people. Through drama the student may explore many social themes. As students contribute through roles a picture of entrenched and conflicting attitudes may emerge which have to be defended on either side. By so doing they absorb and challenge the opposing views by working within and through the symbolic situation. In dramatising a social theme, meaning becomes clearer and attitudes may be modified and sometimes changed. For example, in an improvisation about whether a doctor was right or wrong to turn off the life support machine of a woman who had suffered severe brain damage in a car accident, the students had held very definite views in the preliminary discussions: the majority thought it was morally wrong to let the woman die. However, after acting out the situation and becoming aware of the pain and suffering of the woman's husband and children, some of the students actually changed their view. The symbolic situation can be used as a vehicle through which we can determine issues and their underlying problems. Through drama we can explore important social issues and, perhaps, re-evaluate our own attitudes towards them while beginning to understand those of other people.

In helping a student to develop skills through the medium of drama we extend abilities in the use of the process itself for exploring problems of meaning, and we broaden her dramatic vocabulary so that she may be able to express and communicate her ideas in a more satisfying way.

Development through social interaction in drama focuses primarily on the simultaneous symbolic and real relationships of people, the roles they play, personalities, feelings and ideas and the human situation in which they find themselves. Drama is effective as a means of communicating ideas and feelings to other people and the student learns how to put ideas across clearly.

The role of the teacher

Teaching drama is not like teaching any other subject, perhaps because it is not really a subject but rather a creative process. In some aspects this is also true of ESL. The subject teacher possesses a body of knowledge and

---

6. Many people learn to operate on a bi-cultural level and gain advantages from both cultures by being able to manipulate both. This may involve moving between two class cultures, for example, of the native speaker or two ethnic cultures for the non-native speaker.

her role is to impart that knowledge to her students. The students know what to expect; they know what their short-term and their long-term goals are. They may be working through a syllabus in which each stage of learning is clearly defined. The teacher has control over their learning and although a variety of teaching methods may be used the ultimate aim is to make the students proficient in the subject being learned. The drama teacher, however, is concerned with creating a learning environment and she shares the learning process with the students. Her role is to stimulate the students, not to instruct them.

Often the initial response of students to drama is one of suspicion or fear and sometimes they need to be convinced that it is 'good for them'. On the surface it may appear to be a somewhat frivolous and self-indulgent activity and it is essential that the teacher manifests a belief that what they are doing has value and meaning. To achieve this she must appear to be committed to drama, confident and enthusiastic. Total involvement is essential. It is no good providing an initial stimulus and then leaving the students to get on with it because they won't.

At the beginning of a drama course I usually spend a little time talking about the theory of using drama with the students and explaining the ways in which I think it can help them. Some will be convinced, but others will make a judgement based on their own experience of the lesson so the teacher must work hard to involve them and leave them with a positive feeling about the work they are engaged in, otherwise the classroom will be empty the following week.

The beginning of the lesson is of paramount importance as the initial atmosphere you create will influence what follows. Careful planning is essential, and that must include the physical organisation of the classroom. If you start with warm-up exercises, for example, make sure that sufficient space has been made and that the students have adequate room in which to move freely.

Be sure you know exactly what you are going to do as any dithering or hesitation will put the students off and you will lose their attention. It is essential that interest is aroused from the outset and maintained.

Since for many students drama may be unfamiliar and perhaps threatening it is important not to throw them in at the deep end, but to establish a safe and secure atmosphere in which they can experiment and make discoveries about themselves and each other. Developing confidence is a gradual process and the teacher needs to train herself in observation of the class in order to assess the capability of the individual student. Don't do what an acting teacher did to me once in my first class – 'Go up on the stage and pretend you are a patient in a mental hospital'! In the following chapters I have suggested a programme of warm-up and relaxation exercises, mime and movement activities and drama games which will help to develop the students confidence and will prepare them for dramatic role-play and improvisation. It is inadvisable to try class-room drama without these preliminary stages. If a student is placed in a situation where she is vulnerable and exposed and has not been trained to handle the situation she will be loth to return.

This is not to suggest that the teacher should impose limitations on the students and shield them from challenging role-play and improvisation. I am continually amazed at students' ability to handle complex and sophisticated ideas and language, and there is a danger of teachers underestimating the students' potential, but they should not be challenged before they are ready.

One useful way into stimulating drama is when the teacher works 'in role', that is directing the action as a character within it; this will be described in following chapters. The advantage of this method is that a more dynamic relationship with the students may be established. 'In role' she can be challenging, provocative, aggressive or subversive and tease out appropriate responses from the students. In one improvisation about women in prison in which I was playing the role of a particularly obnoxious person a student who was normally rather timid and self-effacing launched a bitter attack on me and properly put me in my place! Her voice became louder and stronger and she spoke fluently and with confidence. She was acting out her role but she was also revealing part of herself which through shyness and lack of confidence was usually kept hidden. For the student it was a sort of break-through and she was never quite so timid again. For the teacher it was evidence that performing drama can change people.

The teacher 'in role' can also provide a focus and she can manipulate a situation and affect what is happening in the improvisation and make it more significant.

Finally, drama should not be all action. Time should be spent discussing and reflecting on the work done and analysing and evaluating the content.

3
Warm-up and relaxation exercises

Warm-up and relaxation exercises

It is important to establish a simple routine of warm-up and relaxation exercises at the beginning of each lesson and these exercises should not be rushed through or regarded as a waste of time. Students will arrive at their drama class in various states of mind and physical condition based on their recent experiences. Are they listless or lively, relaxed or tense, sleepy or wide awake, in good or bad humour? Since drama is a group activity and active participation is essential, it is as well to prepare the group psychologically for the work they are going to do, and a few simple physical exercises will serve to relax the tense student and enliven the languid one.

Five or ten minutes spent in this way will put the student at ease, in the right frame of mind for drama and help to create a group feeling. Although the exercises are mostly non-verbal, the students will be practising their listening skills as they follow your instructions and later, when these exercises are familiar to them, you may ask a student to lead this introductory session and gain practice in giving commands. Some exercises involve physical contact and this helps to break down barriers and make students feel more comfortable with each other. Unless students feel relaxed and safe as a group it is almost impossible for any drama to take place.

How many exercises you do must be a personal choice based on your knowledge of your students and what seems appropriate at the time. Much will depend on the length of the lesson and how frequently you meet the students. Some exercises, particularly in the movement and mime section, may be seen as appropriate preparation for an improvisation or role play that you are planning to do later in the lesson. I would suggest that the 'limbering' exercises are always included at the beginning of the lesson and that two or three other exercises are chosen before embarking on the drama aspect of the class.

These exercises should be found suitable for all levels, since they are mostly non-verbal, but you will have to use your judgement about when to introduce those involving physical contact, as some people are very inhibited about touching each other. However, if you introduce them in a matter-of-fact, unselfconscious way and also participate yourself the students usually will be quite happy to follow suit. Never force anyone to do something they clearly feel unhappy about.

1. Limbering

Method:
Clear room of furniture as far as possible.
If you have access to a hall so much the better.

Tell students to remove shoes but do not insist and find a space in the room facing you.
Talk the students through these exercises slowly, repeating when necessary and demonstrating at the same time.

Shake and stretch.
Shake fingers on left hand, shake wrist, lower arm, upper arm, shoulder.
Repeat sequence with right arm.
Shake left toes, foot, leg, thigh, hip.
Repeat with right leg.
Shake whole body and head.
Stretch arms above head and try to touch the ceiling, let go and drop arms and torso to the floor.
Swing arms backwards and forwards through legs.
Come up slowly, arms at the sides.
Raise left arm above head and bend over to touch right foot.
Repeat twice and then do the same with right arm.
Imagine you are standing in a box. Try to touch all the corners above and below.
Swing hips and roll, shrug shoulders and roll, stretch face and contract, tense arms and relax, tense legs and relax, tense whole body and relax.
Rub surfaces of arms, face, legs and thighs.
Run on the spot up to the count of ten.
Imagine you are trapped in a huge bubble – push, punch and kick to get out.

Comment:
These are not very demanding exercises physically and everyone should be capable of doing them. They will serve to get the blood circulation moving, to ease tension and make the students aware of their bodies. There is no need to stick rigidly to the above. Students can be asked to suggest variations and additions but don't include anything too strenuous. This is not a keep-fit class!

2. Neck massage and back rub

Method:
Ask the students to find a partner and in turn give each other a neck massage and a back rub.
Alternatively this can be done in a line, with each person giving a massage and receiving one at the same time.
The first person in the line will only be receiving, unless the exercise is done in a circle.

Comment:
The first time you do this exercise there will probably be some giggling and embarrassment if the students are not used to touching each other, but talk them through the exercise, pointing out how the neck is often a centre of tension and how gentle manipulation can be very beneficial and pleasant. Make sure you participate in the exercise. It may be the teacher's view that exercises involving physical contact such as the above are not appropriate for a particular group. If in doubt leave them out.

3. Group exercises

Method:
1. *Group stretch:* stand in circle holding hands, gradually move back as far as possible, keeping hold of each other's hands, into a group stretch and yawning loudly at the same time.
2. *Group shapes:* stand in groups of three or four holding hands, feet firm on the ground, but allow body and arms to move the group into different shapes on different levels, high and low.
3. *Free fall:* in groups of five, four students form a circle and the fifth one stands in the middle, eyes closed. The student in the middle allows herself to sway forward, sideways and backwards and the other students catch her and push her gently back to an upright position. Keep feet firmly in one place. Each student takes a turn in the middle. Make sure nobody falls down as this would defeat the purpose of the exercise, which is one of establishing trust.
4. *Group sculpture:* one student takes up a pose and each student in turn attaches herself to make a group shape. It doesn't have to represent anything in particular – it can be an abstract shape. Alternatively one student uses the bodies of the others, placing their arms and legs in different positions to make a group sculpture.
5. *Group knot:* students link hands and stand in a line. The leader weaves in and out of the line gradually creating a knot, or several knots. Hands must be held tightly throughout the exercise and the chain must not be broken. When the group is completely 'tied up' the leader must unravel this human knot by retracing her steps.
6. *Copying a movement:* students stand in a circle one foot apart and one student makes a movement, like a dance step, for example. Everyone copies, then the next student repeats the first movement and adds another and again everyone copies and so on until everyone has added a movement.
(You may end up with a nice dance routine!)

Comment:
The main purpose of these group exercises is to build up a feeling of mutual confidence and co-operation. Drama involves taking risks and this can only be done in an atmosphere of trust. In exercises involving physical contact trust can begin to develop and students will feel relaxed and safe with each other.

The next three exercises are really games, since they contain an element of competition and are rule-bound, but I have included them in this section as they are non-verbal and involve physical effort.

Method:
1. *Jumping ball game:* the students form a circle with one student in the middle and the object is to hit the student's feet with the ball. When the student is hit she leaves the circle and is replaced by another. The student in the middle can move around and jump to avoid being hit by the ball.
   If you have a large group you can put half in the middle and the rest in the circle. Their task is to eliminate the others one by one. The one left in the middle is the winner.
2. *Rolling ball game:* students stand in a circle, feet slightly apart and touching person next to them. A ball is rolled across the circle and the object is not to let it pass through the legs but to push it back in different directions across the floor. When it rolls through, that particular student is out and the circle closes up until everyone is out.
3. *Passing a rhythm* (accompanied by a movement): students sit in a circle and one person leaves the room. One person is chosen to lead the group. Every movement they make, hand-clapping for example, is taken up by the whole group. The person who left the room returns and stands in the middle of the circle. Her task is to discover who is changing the movement in the group. When she has guessed the right person, someone else is chosen.
4. *Murder by winking:* this game is similar to the one described above. Someone is asked to leave the room and someone else is chosen to be 'murderer'. The murderer must wink at his victims. When the murderer winks the person winked at must pretend to die and the person who was outside must try to guess who is doing the winking. This game gives plenty of scope for dramatic falls and students usually enjoy it.
5. *What's missing:* one person leaves the room and takes off something they were wearing or changes something about their appearance. When they come back the rest of the group must try to discover what is different.

Comment:
The main object of playing these games is again to establish group co-operation. The games are also concerned with concentration and observation, which are essential skills to be developed.

4. Working in pairs

Method:
1. *Mirroring:* students stand facing a partner with their hands raised to shoulder height, palms facing outward and as close to their partner as possible without actually touching. One student is the 'leader' and begins to move both hands and arms to make shapes in different directions. The partner must follow the movements as closely as possible as though they were mirror reflections.
2. *Hand touching:* this exercise is similar to mirroring, but this time the students close their eyes, the palms of their hands actually touching and they move together as one.
3. *Matchstick:* in pairs standing opposite a partner, students hold a matchstick between two index fingers and gradually move their hands and then arms as freely as possible without dropping the matchstick. Swap hands.
4. *See-saw:* in pairs, sit on floor facing each other, holding hands and pull and push backwards and forwards like a see-saw, slowly feeling the weight of your partner.
5. *Shapes:* in pairs one student stands still and allows partner to move her into different shapes. Try five shapes each and give each shape a name.

Comment:
Try to ensure when doing paired work that students don't stick always to the same partner. I usually do this by saying 'Now find someone with the same coloured eyes as you have' or 'Find someone with different coloured shoes to yours.' The object is to get the students used to working with each other.[7] The first three exercises are particularly good for developing concentration and could be accompanied by music if possible. Eye contact is another feature of these exercises which is an important aspect of communication.

---

7. It is necessary to establish rapport with one person before real group integration is possible.

5. Blind exercises

Method:
1. Group form a circle, one person goes into the middle and closes her eyes. Another person goes into the middle. First person tries to guess who it is by touch. Must not speak.
2. In pairs. One person to shut eyes and be led round the room by the other. Put plenty of objects around the room that can be touched and identified. This exercise can be done silently and the students can discuss afterwards what they have touched or they can identify the objects when they touch them. The student leading may ask them questions: Is it hard or soft? Smooth or rough? What do you think it is made of?
3. In pairs, A chooses a sound, e.g. a low whistle, a hand-clap, for B to identify. All the Bs stand at one end of the room and the As move about freely. Bs must close their eyes and go towards the sound which As make repeatedly as they move around the room. When they have found their partners they change over.
4. Sitting in a circle each student in turn is asked to close eyes and is then given an object to try to identify by touch. The other students may ask them questions: Is it made of plastic? Is it large or small? Alternatively you can ask the student to describe the object: This object is very small. It's made of glass or plastic. It feels like a bottle shape. It's got a screw top. The contents are liquid. It smells nice. I think it's a bottle of perfume.
5. Listening to sounds in the room and outside. All the students sit down and close their eyes and just listen. You may add some noises if the environment is very quiet or play a pre-recorded tape of various sounds. After a few minutes students open their eyes and tell you what they have heard.
6. In pairs, A closes eyes and B makes three distinctive sounds using objects: rattle of keys, filing of nails, brushing hair, counting money. B tries to identify them, then change over.

Comment:
These are all useful discrimination exercises analogous with verbal discrimination which help to develop concentration and sensitivity to the environment. Give the students an opportunity to discuss how they felt while doing them. The answers can be quite interesting.

4
Movement and mime

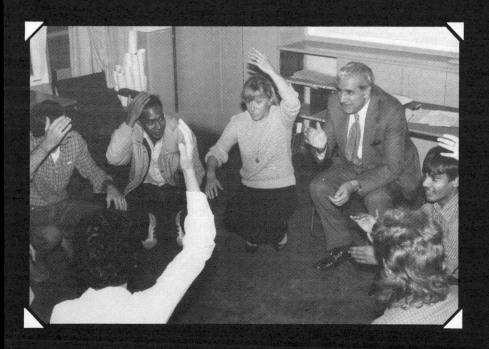

Most of these activities are non-verbal, but they do in fact involve considerable language work in terms of listening, comprehension and discussion. They also serve as an introduction to drama in a non-threatening way, as participation is not dependent solely on linguistic skills, and they can help the student to develop an awareness of the para-language, which is often culturally and socially based, and an awareness of their own body language. Communication exists in many forms and the way in which we express ourselves through gesture, facial and body movements is a great indicator of our feelings and attitudes.

Again, I would suggest that two or three of these activities are chosen to follow the warm-up and relaxation session. Some may be found to be useful preparation for a particular role-play or improvisation.

Although most of the activities are non-verbal a good passive knowledge of English would be necessary in order to follow the instructions. It would, however, be possible to simplify some of them to use with beginners and elementary students.

1. Ways of moving – responding to different physical conditions

Method:
Tell the students to find a space in the room and start moving around according to your instructions. You will need to get them imaginatively involved by the way you talk them through the activity.

Do not participate in the activity, because you really need to watch what they are doing, but demonstrate if you feel the meaning of the words is not clear.

Talking through:
- Move around the room very *slowly* – imagine it is very hot and humid, you have no energy, your limbs feel very heavy, your feet are like concrete, the sun is beating down on your head.
- Move very *quickly,* it's very cold, you are shivering, your coat is very thin, you feel chilled to the bone, the wind and rain are lashing you. You are in a great hurry to get home.
- Move very *heavily* – you are going up a hill and you are carrying heavy suitcases. Your arms are aching.
- Move very *lightly* – you feel light and airy, almost weightless, your feet are hardly touching the ground, you are almost floating on soft white clouds.
- Walking in a thick fog
- Walking in very high-heeled shoes

- Walking through mud in heavy boots
- Walking over ice
- Walking on hot stones on the beach barefoot
- Carrying full cups or glasses
- Walking along a tightrope
- Walking along a ledge with a sheer drop on one side
- Walking through a minefield in the dark
- Climbing a rockface
- Walking with a fierce dog on a leash
- Walking with a pot on your head
- Following someone but trying not to be seen
- Being followed and feeling nervous
- Walking through water up to your waist
- Walking with eyes closed.

Comment:
Do not attempt to do all these movements in one lesson. Four or five should be sufficient. If you try to do more the students will become confused and the activity will lose its point. The aim is to get the students to concentrate and really think about what they are doing and how the physical conditions may affect the way they move.

Get the students to discuss how they felt about what they were doing, for example, walking with a fierce dog: 'I felt I was being pulled along. I had no control over my movements. I was afraid I would fall over. My arm was aching.'

2. Ways of moving

Method:
Give the students a list of verbs of movement. These can be written on the board or given to them individually on cards: e.g. limp, stride, skip, jump, hop, stagger, push, pull, drag, tiptoe, creep, swing, slide, shuffle etc. Ask the students to demonstrate these verbs and then say when they would move in this way. For example, limp – 'I would limp if I had hurt my foot.'

Comment:
This activity gives lots of opportunity for language practice. It could be made into a guessing-game where the students have to observe each other and then guess which verbs they were demonstrating.

3. Moving in different moods

In this exercise the students are asked to express emotions through movement. Later, through role-play and improvisation, they will have an opportunity to express their emotions in speech as well as movement.

Method:
1. Talk the students through the exercise and get them to think about what they are doing.
   Ask the students to find a space in the room and begin moving about in:
   - A happy, relaxed mood
   - nervous, twitchy
   - confident, self-assured
   - worried, anxious
   - depressed
   - shy, embarrassed
   - aggressive, cocky
   - excited
   - angry
   - weary
   - impatient
   - indecisive
   - sad
   - timid, hesitant
   - patient
   - decisive
   - lively
   - friendly
   - hostile
   - dreamy, trance-like

   NB As you work through the exercise it may become apparent that some students do not know the meaning of all of these words. Use the exercise for initial teaching by demonstrating the meanings through movement yourself or getting students who do know to do it. Give the students time at the end of the activity to write words down.

   As you talk the students through the exercise suggest reasons why they might be feeling in a particular mood, for example, shy, embarrassed. 'You have just arrived at a party to which you have been invited but you didn't realise it was formal dress and you are wearing the wrong clothes. Also you don't know anyone there.'

   - Now ask the students to get into pairs and give A a mood to demonstrate from the above list and ask B to choose its opposite, for example, relaxed–nervous, confident–shy, happy–sad. Ask the students to move around the room again and at some point meet up with their partner and exchange a greeting and start a conversation which will express their moods:

Happy: Hello, how are you? Isn't it a lovely day?
Sad: Oh, hello.
Happy: What's wrong? You don't seem very cheerful.
Sad: No, I'm not.
Happy: But why, the sun is shining and it's lovely and warm. I feel really great today.
Sad: I don't.

It may be helpful to suggest a context to the students. For example 'confident' could meet 'shy' at a party or 'impatient' could be waiting to be served in a shop by 'patient', who is very slow.

- Continuing the theme of expressing mood through movement, ask students to get into pairs again and ask A to express a mood and B to watch and then try to copy the movement. The students then discuss what they were doing and B tries to put into words what she has observed.

4. Moving as different types of people – comparisons and opposites

Method:
Working in pairs, give each pair a card with a description of two types of person written on it:
old person – young person
tall – short
straight – twisted
stiff – loose
busy – lazy
gentle – rough
fat person – thin person
light – heavy
beautiful – ugly
strong – weak
friendly – cold
quiet – noisy
Ask the students to move about the room trying to convey the type of person written on their card and then to meet up with their partner and exchange a greeting.

5. Occupations

> **Method:**
> Ask the students to choose an occupation which involves movement and, in pairs, try to guess what the partner does. If the student can't think of an occupation give her one written on a piece of paper to try: for example, policeman, model, dancer, athelete, boxer, soldier, tramp, waiter, milkman, postman, traffic warden, fireman, etc.

Comment:
Through all these movement activities one is slowly preparing the students for drama. They are beginning to think about feelings and how to express them; they are beginning to think about role and characterisation. By concentrating on the para-linguistic features of language one is helping the student to interpret the signals of non-verbal communication and to respond appropriately.

Mime

It may seem a little odd to the language teacher that mime should feature prominently in drama for the second language learner, but it is an important aspect for a variety of reasons. As with movement it emphasises the para-linguistic features of communication such as facial expression, gesture and non-verbal sound; it is confidence-building, enabling the students to get up and do things in front of each other and, since there is little or no language involved in the performance of the mime, it is non-threatening to the student who lacks verbal confidence; it also aids the development of imagination, observation and concentration and helps to extend the students' emotional range. Mime is also a source of great enjoyment and I have observed that students tend to be very enthusiastic about this aspect of drama. There is in fact plenty of language practice too for the students who are watching and guessing a mime.

1. Using an object

> **Method:**
> Take an object, for example, a hammer, and ask students, in turn, to mime an action using the object. This can be done with the students standing in a circle and the student who is performing the mime going into the middle.
> The class try to guess what the object has become, for example:
> cleaning teeth – it's a toothbrush
> hitting a ball – it's a bat
> holding to ear – it's a telephone

2. What are you doing?

Method:
Someone goes into the middle of the circle, probably the teacher the first time, and mimes an action,
e.g. brushing hair.
Someone steps forward from the circle and says: 'What are you doing?'
The first person says something different from what they are doing:
e.g. 'I'm cleaning my teeth.'
Second person then mimes what the first person says and then when asked 'What are you doing?' says something different.
Repeat until everyone in the circle has had a turn.

3. Occupations

Method:
This is a simple guessing game. Each student in turn mimes the actions involved in a particular occupation and the others must guess what she is doing. Once they have guessed, ask the student to repeat the mime, this time describing what she is doing at each stage.
A variation on this game is to ask the students to work in pairs. A mimes an occupation and B copies what she sees and then the two students discuss what they were doing.

4. Subjects for mime

Method:
Give students a subject for mime on a card or if they prefer they can choose their own subject.
● surgeon performing an operation
● tramp looking for cigarette butts in the gutter
● laying the table for a dinner party
● a pickpocket at work
● making an omelette
● milking a cow
● feeding birds in the park
● an animal in a cage at the zoo
● decorating a room
● changing a plug

- making a cup of tea
- house cleaning
- a barber giving someone a shave
- changing a baby's napkin
- changing a wheel on a car
- window-dressing
- postman delivering letters
- looking for a lost contact lens
- working on an assembly line in a factory
- fishing.

Again, after each mime you can ask the student to repeat the mime and to describe each stage of her mime or ask the class to describe it.

5. Messages

Method:
In two groups work out a short scene based on the theme 'unspoken messages':
e.g. policeman directing traffic and people
men at a fire station receiving a call out
hooter in a factory signal to stop working.
Five minutes to prepare scene and then one group shows the other group who tries to guess what its about.

Comment:
These are simple activities which can be done even with elementary students. The students will gain confidence by doing things in front of each other and they will be learning to think 'on their feet' and to develop their imaginations. They are also exercises in observation and concentration.

6. Guess what's in the parcel

Method:
In pairs, students imagine one of them has received a parcel. Can the partner guess what is in it from the way the parcel is opened, what she does with the contents and her response to the parcel. For example, it might be a case of wine, or a beautiful dress. Then they swap roles and afterwards talk about it with the group.

7. Good or bad news?

Method:
Students work in pairs. Imagine one of them has received a letter or a telegram containing news. Can partner guess what sort of news it is from her response?
e.g. delighted, excited, fairly pleased, disappointed, upset, angry, frustrated etc.

Comment:
Nos. 6 and 7 are good exercises for practising facial expressions as a means of communication.

8. Emotions to mime

Method:
This activity may involve the students working in groups of two or three and they will need five minutes to discuss what they are going to do and an opportunity to have a run-through before they show it to the group. The situation should be presented on cards for the students to study in their groups and it should be explained that you want them to concentrate on the sequence of emotions shown on the card and to show how their emotions change as the situation changes:

SUSPICION

PANIC

RELIEF (two persons)

You are in bed. It's the middle of the night. You wake up and you think you can hear a noise downstairs. You listen. You hear the sound of a window being forced and then footsteps on the stairs and then you get into a panic.
Suddenly your bedroom door opens slowly. It's your husband/son. He has been away and he has returned home unexpectedly a day early and he had lost his key so he climbed in through the window.

WEARINESS

GRATITUDE

HORROR (two persons)

You are carrying several heavy packages. You are very tired and your arms ache. A stranger stops and offers to help you. You are very pleased and thank the stranger but then he suddenly runs off with one of the packages and leaves you helpless on the roadside.

PLEASURE

IMPATIENCE

HORROR (two persons)

You are happily preparing the table for dinner. You are expecting your husband home soon. Time passes and he doesn't arrive. You begin to get impatient. The dinner is spoiling. Suddenly there is a knock at the door but it is not your husband. It's a policeman with bad news. Your husband has been hurt in a car accident.

IMPATIENCE

RELIEF

ANGER (three or more persons)

You have been waiting for a bus for nearly one hour. It's very cold and wet. You are getting very impatient. Suddenly you see a bus coming in the distance and you are very pleased. It arrives and people get on but the conductor stops you. No more room. You argue but it makes no difference. The bus goes on and you are very angry.

BOREDOM

EXCITEMENT

FRUSTRATION (one person)

You are at home alone feeling very bored. You put on the T.V. – nothing interesting so you turn it off. You pick up a book – it's boring too. You don't know what to do. The phone rings – a friend is inviting you to a party now. You are very excited. You get ready. Get into your car but it won't start. You investigate but can't get it to start. You feel very frustrated.

NERVOUSNESS

DISAPPOINTMENT

ANGER (three persons)

You are waiting for an interview for a job. Your friend is waiting too. You feel very nervous but your friend is very calm. You are called in first. You return feeling very disappointed as you don't think you did very well. You wait for your friend who goes in next. The friend is successful. You are very angry. You think you should have got the job.

DEPRESSION

APPREHENSION

PLEASURE (two persons)

You are feeling very low. Suddenly there is a knock on the door. It's the postman with a telegram – you sign for it. You are afraid to open it in case it's bad news. You feel very apprehensive. You open it and it's good news. Your boyfriend/girlfriend will be arriving in one hour after six months abroad.

N.B. While the students are preparing go round the groups and make sure they understand everything written on the card and especially the emotions you want them to convey.

Comment:
This activity will give the students further practice in conveying emotion through non-verbal means, that is, facial expressions, body language, non-verbal sounds; it will also develop a feeling for the need for preparation, climax and resolution in all types of work. Later these role cards can be used again with language when the emphasis will be on revealing the meaning through words. This particular exercise would be suitable for fairly advanced groups.
Variation/development. Use the mood words. Students improvise their own situations.

9. Moods

Students have to think of a mood or state, or they can be given one on a piece of paper: for example, anger, hunger, boredom, anxiety, fear, tiredness. They must try to convey the mood only through gestures and facial and body expressions. This may be done individually or a student can choose a partner if another person is needed in the scene. If any of the students are devoid of ideas, try to help them. For example, fear: 'Can you think of a situation in which you would be frightened? Would you be frightened if you were stuck in a lift, for example, or if there was a big spider in your room?'
The other students can be asked to guess what the mood was.

10. In the mood

Method:
Give the students a list of adverbs describing manner, for example, happily, clumsily, aggressively, tentatively, noisily, miserably, resentfully, eagerly, etc. Then tell them to do things choosing one of the moods on the list:
Open the window
Walk across the room
Pick something up.
The class guess which mood they are in from the way each student carries out the action.
Variation: One student leaves the room. The class are then given an adverb, for example, 'enthusiastically'.
The student comes back and gives the class various orders and they all carry out the actions in that mood until the first student guesses what it is.

Comment:
In the last two activities one is still concerned with conveying feelings and attitudes through non-verbal means, but in this last activity there is plenty of scope for language development. Both would be suitable for elementary students, providing that the verbs and adverbs chosen were fairly simple ones.

11. Copying mime

Method:
One person goes out in front, picks a simple activity to mime and begins doing it. Other players go out one at a time and join him in this activity. When all the students have joined in ask each one to write down what he thought he was doing, then the first person reveals what he was doing: for example, scrubbing a floor, painting a wall.

12. What am I?

Method:
One student goes out in front and starts an activity related to an occupation, for example: surgeon.
Other students join her when they think they know what she is doing and begin an action related to her activity, for example: nurse, patient, anaesthetist.
After the activity is established tell the students to add speech.

13. Slow motion

Method:
Ask the students to perform an activity in pairs in slow motion.
When they have practised their mime ask each pair to show the
group and the group to say what they were doing.

14. Speeded up

Method:
As above but this time the activity is speeded up like an old film.

15. Robots

Method:
In pairs ask the students to choose one to be a robot and the other
to dictate orders. A tells B to perform various domestic chores as
though she was a robot, for example:
clean the windows
make the bed
prepare my bath.

16. Master/slave

Method:
Again in pairs, A is master, B is slave. A gives orders to B. They
may be simple activities to perform or just arbitrary actions, for
example: put your hands on your head, touch your toes, etc. Then
they change over.
Next ask students to get into groups of three and label them A, B
and C. This time A has two slaves. Repeat activity. Then groups
of four and so on until the whole group is involved in one activity.

Comment:
Activities numbered 11–16 are suitable for beginners and elementary
students as the verbal content is minimal, but they are also good for
building confidence and getting the students to use their bodies in a
number of different ways.

17. Idioms and proverbs

Method:
Give students an idiom or proverb to look at on a piece of paper.
It may be necessary to explain the meaning individually to the
students first. They must then try to convey the words on the
paper by acting out what is described so that the remainder of the
group can try to guess what is written on the paper. This can be
done with mime and some verbal clues if necessary.
The students can use other members of the group to help in the
mime.
Variation: Get students to suggest proverbs from their own
language which they can translate.
Suggested idioms and proverbs
flogging a dead horse
she gave him the cold shoulder
I'm out of my depth
he's very tight-fisted
to wear one's heart on one's sleeve
you give me a pain in the neck
too may cooks spoil the broth
under the thumb
fish out of water
make haste while the sun shines
don't put all your eggs in one basket
out of the frying-pan into the fire
haven't got a leg to stand on
I wouldn't like to be in your shoes
don't make a mountain out of a molehill
no use crying over spilt milk
keep it under your hat
'tongue in cheek
it's on the tip of my tongue
he has a chip on his shoulder
pride comes before a fall
you can't pull the wool over my eyes.

When the students have got the gist of the idiom write it on the
board and then ask them to try to decide what it means in plain
English, for example:
keep it under your hat – don't tell anyone

Comment:
Obviously there are hundreds more to choose from and students may
have a particular favourite of their own. 'Raining cats and dogs' is a

popular one! Students usually enjoy learning idioms and find many of them very amusing so it is a good exercise to stimulate interest. It is suitable only for very advanced students and native speakers and gives them useful practice in observation and communication.

18. Chain mime

Method:
Five people are chosen to leave the room. The group then decides on a mime sequence for them to do, for example: making a complicated sandwich, changing a baby's nappy.
A is called in and told what to do
B is then called in and watches while A mimes something
C is then called in and B repeats what he saw A do
C repeats the mime for D, D repeats for E
E mimes it for the audience. The usual result is that the mime changes with each repetition, so that E is doing something entirely different.
Ask each person what he thought he was doing.

Comment:
A good exercise for concentration and memorisation.

5
Voice

The first function of speech is, of course, communication and when teaching English, especially as a second language, the teacher is therefore primarily concerned with intelligibility. Pronunciation is an important aspect of the language learning process and students need much practice in the sounds and stresses of the language in order to modify their accents and render themselves intelligible in all forms of communication. It is a fact, however, that many students seem to remain somewhat unintelligible, not because of accent or faulty pronunciation, but because they do not use the voice correctly. Clarity of diction depends not only on correct formation of sounds but on good articulation and audibility. Muffled speech, indistinctness and inaudibility may be caused by various physical reasons such as closed mouths, lazy lips and lazy tongues which may in turn be rooted in psychological conditions, such as lack of confidence. If one is reluctant to speak or uncertain about the correctness of one's speech this will affect the muscles involved in making speech. Often the second language learner may try to hide faulty grammar either by talking very softly and hoping mistakes will not be heard or speaking very fast and hoping they will pass unnoticed. On the other hand, speech may be intelligible, articulation and projection good but the voice is grating on the ear, harsh or excessively nasal or too high pitched. These faults may be due to some physical constriction or tension in the resonators or it could also be due to lack of confidence.[8]

We can compare the voice to a machine which consists of many parts which must all work together in harmony. If the machine is to work efficiently we must be aware of pitch, projection, tonality, texture, resonance and breath control. But unlike any other machine the voice can express emotions. It is not only a means of communication but also an expression of our individual personality and there are many factors, both physical and psychological, which have contributed to its making. The voice is a powerful instrument and we are affected and influenced by the quality of a person's voice sometimes even more than by the actual words they are speaking. It is possible for someone to stroke you with the voice and stab you with the words simultaneously!

An attractive, well-modulated voice is a great asset in winning friends and influencing people. We grow impatient with a mumbler whose speech is inaudible; we grow bored with a dull, monotonous, unvarying tone; we shut our ears to a harsh or whining voice and a shrill or booming voice may cause offence, but we may be charmed and won by a voice which has a tone and texture that is smooth and pleasing to the ear. A pleasant voice that is open and reveals the personality can be very persuasive.

Good speech then depends on various aspects of voice production and the purpose of this chapter is to consider some of them and to suggest a

---

8. There may also be a different use of voice because of differences demanded by the native language.

few exercises and activities that could be used to increase the students' awareness of the voice and to help them become more flexible and confident in the use of speech: there is only space here to introduce the subject of voice and draw attention to the importance of the quality of speech. For the teacher interested in doing intensive voice work with her students there are many books on speech training which provide a comprehensive programme of exercises for relaxation and breathing, clarity of diction and vocal flexibility. *Your Voice and How to Use It Successfully* by Cicely Berry is a good example.

Breathing

Correct breathing is essential to good speech. Many people breathe and produce their voices naturally and well by habit. A large breath confined to the lower chest is inhaled without effort and then exhaled in a steady flow. In some people, however, breathing is too shallow or they lack control over the rate of flow. In this case they may need to take air in the middle of a sentence or, when speaking over a long period, they may run out of air and finish in a state of breathlessness which results in inaudibility at the end of sentences. These faults can be eliminated by exercises designed to improve inspiration and the control of expiration.

Method:
1. Tell students to stand or lie in a relaxed position. Place hands, palms inward on the front of the waist so that fingers are almost touching. If breathing correctly they will feel a tensing of the diaphragm and fingers will move apart indicating correct lateral movement of the lower ribs. Do not raise shoulder blades. Gradually increase the depth of breathing.
2. Inhale quickly through the nose and exhale slowly through the mouth.
3. Inhale slowly through the nose and exhale quickly through the mouth.
4. Imitate a yawn. Softly and lazily say a prolonged 'AH!'
5. Inhale to count of four; hold the breath for four; exhale to four. Gradually increase the count to twenty. Teacher should do the counting.
6. Inhale, hold the breath for two, exhale to the sound of 'MOO' for a count of four. Concentrate on making the volume of the sound steady throughout. Repeat this using other sounds. Increase the count.
7. Inhale and say:
   "I went to the cinema yesterday.'

Inhale again and say:
'I went to the cinema yesterday with my friend Ben.'
Repeat:
'I went to the cinema yesterday with my friend Ben and his brother Bill.'
Repeat:
'I went to the cinema yesterday with my friend Ben and his brother Bill and we saw a very good film.'
Repeat:
'I went to the cinema yesterday with my friend Ben and his brother Bill and we saw a very good film at the Odeon cinema in Hammersmith.'

Record the last sentence and listen for any unsteadiness in the flow of speech or breathlessness towards the end. Make up other sentences and lengthen them in a similar manner.

Comment:
These exercises will make students aware of their breathing and the effect it has on the sounds we produce. One or two exercises could be incorporated into the warm-up and relaxation part of the lesson. Relaxed breathing is essential for drama.

Resonance
For developing volume and quality the chief resonators, the mouth, throat and nose have an important effect on the voice. The sound is amplified and made fuller and richer by passing through these hollow spaces.

Method:
1. Ask students to hum in unison concentrating the sound on the back of the throat.
   Gradually increase volume and then let sound fade away.
2. Hum again, this time concentrating sound directly under the dome-shape of the hard palate. Gradually increase volume and then let sound fade away. You should experience a tickling sensation on the lips.
   Notice the different sounds produced by vibrating the air in different places.
3. Hum again and then open mouth and sound 'AH!' without losing any mouth resonance.
4. Repeat 3. with different combinations of consonants and vowels, e.g. n and aw; m and oo; n and ee, a and ng.

Comment:
The purpose of these exercises is to give the students a feeling for resonance and to make them aware that they can control volume and tone by vibrating the air in the resonators. Loudness should not be achieved by shouting and straining the voice.

Articulation

Articulation is the muscular process by means of which we modify the voice or breath with tongue, teeth, lips and other speech organs to produce speech sounds. Poor articulation will render speech indistinct or inaudible. Mumbling is the fault of not opening the mouth wide enough.

Exercises for the lower jaw
Method:
1. Open the mouth to its fullest extent. Repeat action opening and closing a number of times. If you hear a clicking sound continue until it ceases.
2. Open mouth, shape lips and say 'AH!' as in 'father'. Repeat several times.
3. Open mouth, shape lips and say 'EE' as in 'free'. Repeat several times.
4. Say 'AH', 'EE' a number of times paying attention to up-and-down movement of the lower jaw.

Exercises for the lips
Method:
1. Start slowly and gradually increase the pace. Repeat each group of words or syllables at least a dozen times.

papa papa papa papa	mama mama mama mama
baba baba baba baba	wahwah wahwah wahwah
memore memore memore	webe webe webe webe
mypie mypie mypie	bypa bypa bypa bypa

2. Tongue-twisters are a very effective and amusing way of improving the mobility and increasing the agility of the tongue and lips. An excellent book is the anthology of *British Tongue Twisters* by Ken Parkin which includes old favourites like: 'Peter Piper picked a peck of pickled pepper. Where's the peck of pickled pepper Peter Piper picked?'

Comment:
The flexibility of the lips is very important for good articulation, and vowels as well as consonants may suffer from lack of lip mobility.

Exercises for the tongue

Method:

1. Stretch tongue out as far as possible. Pull it back as far as you can. Repeat several times.
2. Try to touch your nose and then your chin with your tongue.
3. Extend tongue and move it from side to side bending the tip in the direction of movement.
4. Move the tip of the tongue from behind the upper teeth, along the middle of the roof of the mouth or hard palate as far back as possible.
5. Repeat the following combinations of sounds, slowly at first and gradually increasing the pace. Repeat each group a number of times.

Tongue-tip and upper teeth ridge   Sounds t d l n r s z

>   tede tede tede   seesaw seesaw seesaw
>   run rat run rat run rat roll rat roll rat
>   ladeda ladeda ladeda   zenzo zenzo zenzo

Back of tongue and soft palate   Sounds k g ng

>   kittykat kittykat kittykat
>   gaga gaga gaga   kegog kegog kegog
>   egging kegging giggling going

Tongue-tip and upper teeth   Sounds th th

>   thick and thin thirty thousand
>   think of three things

Lower lip and upper teeth   Sounds f v

>   feve feve feve   five lives live flies
>   fried fish fish fried vain vi vivain

Tongue blade and front of hard palate   Sounds ch gee sh zh

>   chinchin chopchop chipshop chipshop
>   geegee jojo   jumping jimmy jones
>   shoeshop shipshape sheepshine

Open resonater   Sound h

>   heha hehe heha hahe
>   how horrible his hat

Comment:

The tongue plays an important part in good articulation. Its tip, rear and rim are all involved. The tongue must be agile, supple and capable of stretching. Lack of clarity at the beginning of words and inaudible word endings can often be the fault of a lazy tongue.

Inflexion

Inflexion is the rise and fall of the voice. If a voice is dull and boring it is usually because the inflexion is monotonous. To introduce a greater variety of inflexion one needs to develop the ability to pitch the voice register above and below the normal key. There are books on the subject which attempt to lay down sets of rules for the application of inflexions. *An English Pronouncing Dictionary* by Professor Daniel Jones is an excellent example. The following exercises will give students an opportunity to experiment with inflexion and thereby increase their range.

Method:
1. Count to ten in a level pitch.
   Repeat but this time pitch voice above normal.
   Repeat again pitching voice below normal pitch.
   Speak the numbers beginning 'one' at a low pitch, 'two' at normal, 'three' at high and so on.
   Repeat with days of the week. Names of students in class.
2. Count to ten again but this time say every third number with
   (1) surprise
   (2) impatience
   (3) great pleasure
   (4) anger
   (5) as a question.
   Listen to each other and notice the different inflexions.
3. Say the following sentence in the manner suggested:
   'I don't know what time he will arrive.'
   (1) friendly
   (2) critically
   (3) anxiously
   (4) timidly
   (5) aggressively
   (6) implying you don't care.
6. Try saying the following sentences with different meanings, first lifting one word well above the pitch level, then another.
   'Who did you say you were?'
   'The doctor says there is very little hope.'
   'Well, it is nice of you to come.'

Dramatic Voice Exercises
7. Choose a partner. Each person chooses one word. Have a

friendly chat with partner just using that word. Then using the same word have an angry confrontation with partner.

8. Work out a simple situation to role-play with your partner but try to conduct the conversation in gibberish. After practice each pair show their role-play to the others and they try to guess what it was about. It is surprising how much we may reveal just from inflexion alone.

Other aspects of speech which are important include *pace* which is the rate or speed at which we speak and variation of pace is an aid to inflexion and an interesting voice. *Pause* is also important, not only for the purpose of taking breath but for emphasis and impact. Phrasing too needs to be practised. The best method to practise these skills is, I think, to read short prose extracts and poems aloud with students and to discuss the appropriate phrasing, pace and pause.

Confidence

I suggested earlier that clarity of diction may depend on confidence. If we are relaxed our vocal organs will function as they should and if we are sure of ourselves we tend to speak up clearly and coherently. Many students lack confidence and find it difficult to project their voices or are unwilling to do so. Further activities in speaking in front of each other should help to overcome such problems.

Exercises for confidence

Method:
1. *Verbal boxing*
   Students find a partner. Both speaking at the same time tell your partner in a friendly tone what you have done today from the moment you got up. Change partners and this time tell your partner, again both talking at once, something that you are really angry about.
2. *Flattery*
   In turn tell your partner lots of nice things. Give her as many compliments as you can think of. Then change over.
3. *Reprimands*
   Think of a situation in which you have got to severely reprimand your partner. She must remain silent while you make your criticisms and complaints. Then change over.
4. *Reading stories*
   Find a book of children's fairy stories or stories of adventure. Ask the class to sit in a circle and ask each person in turn to

read aloud from the book. The other students must pretend to be young children so the reader must use her voice to create the excitement and atmosphere of the story.

5. *Inventing stories*

   Ask each student to make up a frightening story lasting about five minutes. It can be about anything at all but entirely fictitious. Give them an opportunity to prepare something and then in turn they tell their story to the group. If any student is unable to invent a story let them read one first and then recall it aloud to the rest of the class.

6. *Poems to recite*

   Give each student a short poem to learn by heart and then recite to the class. These poems should be read aloud in the class and discussed first and then taken away to prepare for the following lesson.

Comment:

All these activities involve using the voice and also thinking about the effect you are trying to achieve with the voice. The voice can have an infinite variety of expression and it is this variety that one wants to make students aware of. We need to give them the confidence to experiment with their voices in order to increase their vocal flexibility.

6
Drama and language games

Games play an important part in drama and language teaching. Not only do they provide a natural introduction to drama, but they are an integral part of the drama lesson for a variety of reasons.

First, they serve as useful preparation. Students must be psychologically prepared for role-play, improvisation and other drama experiences and the game is an excellent way of providing the involvement and personal freedom necessary for experiencing. Through games students can begin to shed their inhibitions and anxieties and their potential is released in the spontaneous effort to meet the demands of the situation.

Games are used in drama schools as a method of training actors in observation, concentration and communication and they may assist in the development of imagination and sensitivity. Although we are primarily concerned with language acquisition, development of these skills will contribute to this end.

In language teaching we are concerned with extending the students word power and increasing fluency, flexibility and agility in the use of English. Games involving concentration, listening, memorisation, observation, discourse, interpretation and interaction can help them to acquire these skills.

In drama teaching the group relationship is of the utmost importance. It depends on a number of individuals working together to complete a given task with full individual participation and personal contribution. If one person dominates there is little pleasure or learning experience for the other members of the group. Through games, which are bound by rules, the students learn the importance of co-operation and interaction with the group. From working within a group the student will acquire confidence and will gradually shed any inhibitions about revealing himself in front of the others. Games help people to relax in groups and break down barriers. Games also provide a secure structure for introducing students to role-play as to some extent the student can protect herself from too much exposure in its format.

The following games have been selected as being relevant to language learners to enable development of the previously mentioned skills. Be careful not to spend the entire lesson playing games, but choose one or two as a preparation for the drama. Also, don't allow the competitive element to predominate. Team games can be adapted to make them non-competitive.

1. Name games

Method (i):
Students stand in a circle and say their names in turn (first names only). Then pick a student to say her name again – the student on

her right side repeats the name and adds her own, the next student repeats both names and says hers and so on round the circle. Obviously it gets more difficult to remember the more names that have to be repeated.

Repeat several times starting at different points in the circle.

Method (ii):
This game would follow on from the first one. Give a small ball to one of the students and ask her to throw it to another student. The student who receives the ball must say the name of the thrower, then they throw it to someone else who must say her name and so on until everyone has had a turn.

Variation:
Throw the ball and say your own name.

Method (iii):
The whole group are asked to move around the room. At a given signal students must move around and shake hands with as many people as possible. With every handshake they are introducing themselves; each person should try to remember as many names as possible.

Comment:
The main purpose of these games is to ensure that the students get to know each others names as this is important in a drama class. The circle is friendly and safe and the games involve lots of eye contact. They are also good memorisation exercises. Suitable for beginners and others.

2. Autobiographies

Method:
Students working in pairs spend about five minutes each giving a personal profile to her partner. Put the following guidelines on the board: name, nationality, education, family, occupation, interests, etc.

The student listening can take brief notes but she just listens – she does not ask questions.

When the As have finished the students then sit in a circle and in turn they play the part of the partner, recalling everything they can remember, for example:

My name is George Kovaks. I'm Hungarian. I'm married. My wife is expecting a baby. etc.

The Bs must listen carefully and report any inaccuracies or omissions when the partner has finished.

Return to pairs and the Bs give their personal details and then repeat the procedure in the circle.
Variation:
Same procedure but this time describing a place.

Comment:
This activity will give the students practice in acquiring several skills: concentration, listening, memorisation and discourse. A teacher suggested to me that some students, especially refugees who may have had bad experiences, would not want to talk about themselves and their lives. I think, however, if you make sure the students know at the beginning that the information will be shared with the whole group they will select what they want to reveal and leave out anything too personal. Most people do enjoy talking about themselves!

3. Identify me

Method:
One person in the group stands with her back to the group and another person describes someone in the group. The student must be careful to describe each person in a positive way, and not in a fashion which could be seen to be derogatory, for example: John is fat and has spots on his face.
Allow a few minutes for the person out in front to guess who is being described. She then chooses another person to come out and the former chooses someone else to describe.

Comment:
A good observation exercise and plenty of language practice involved. The last two games are suitable for post-elementary students.

4. Yes/no game

Method:
The questioner must be a skilled fast talker for this game. Probably the teacher should play this role unless the students are advanced or native speakers.
Each student takes a turn in the 'hot seat' and is bombarded with a series of questions to which he mustn't answer yes or no or shake his head or hesitate, for example:
Do you go to school? I do. Do you smoke? I don't. Did you watch T.V. last night? I didn't. Are you married? I'm not. Did you shake

your head? I didn't.
If the contestant survives one minute of the ordeal he wins. Even
native speakers are usually caught out sooner or later.

Comment:
This game involves concentration and listening skills and, in the case of
the questioner, verbal fluency. Suitable for advanced students.

5. Just a minute

Method:
In this game the student sits out in front and talks for one whole
minute on a given subject. The choice of the subject will depend
on the teacher's knowledge of the student and her level of
competence. For the elementary student one should choose
something fairly concrete, like 'Going shopping' or 'My home',
but to the advanced students one might give an abstract topic like
'Religion' or 'Education'.
The object is for the student to speak fluently for one minute
without drying up or wandering off the subject. A follow-up to
this activity would be to ask the students to write a passage on the
topic that would take one minute to read aloud.
For advanced students or native speakers a version of the radio
panel game 'Just a Minute' might be played in which the student
has to talk for a minute on a given subject without hesitation,
repetition or deviation. For this you would need a stop watch.
When another student catches him or her out she or he takes over
the subject and continues until the minute is up. Suggest a signal
for interrupting, like a hand-clap, for example.

Comment:
This games is very good for practising discourse skills and involves
listening and concentration.

6. Word association

Method:
Students sit or stand in a circle. Give the group a word, for
example, 'hospital'.
Each student has to say a word associated with the word above. It
must fit the category, for example: nurse, doctor, operation,
ward, theatre, etc.

If a student hesitates too long or says a word that doesn't fit the category she leaves the circle. The student who keeps going for the longest time is the winner.

A harder version of this game is to take words from a given category, for example, 'countries', and specify that the last letter of one word must be the first letter of the next, for example:

EnglanD – DenmarK – KenyA – AustraliA

This version requires more thinking time.

Suggested topics:

Food – clothes – cities – schools – offices – holidays – sport – transport – occupations.

7. Alphabet game

Ask students to sit or stand in a circle. Give a letter of the alphabet. Students have to give a word describing an object beginning with the letter until they dry up, for example:

B – baby, book, bread, bed, blanket, bridge, etc.

After playing the game with nouns, try adjectives and verbs.

If a student repeats a word already said or can't supply a word she is out.

8. I like (accumulation)

Method:

Students stand or sit in a circle. One student begins with 'I like something beginning with A', for example:

Food – 'I like apples.'

The next student must say 'I like apples' and something beginning with B, for example: 'I like bread' and so on going through the letters of the alphabet.

I like cake, I like dates, eggs, fish, etc.

Comment:

The last three games can help to develop concentration, listening and memorisation, and will also help to diagnose pronunciation problems. Since the words are said in isolation they must be pronounced correctly to be understood. New vocabulary will arise so stop to explain any words not understood by everyone.

9. Opposites game

Method:

Questioner can ask any questions he chooses which have a yes or

no answer. The contestant may only answer yes or no and must always give the opposite to the true answer, for example:
Is your name John? No
Are you a girl? Yes
Are you wearing a pair of trousers? No
If the contestant fails to give a correct opposite, or does not answer a question within five seconds, she is out. If she survives one minute she wins.

10. Who am I?

Method:
The subject sits in front of the class; the object of the game is for the class to question her and guess what person she is thinking of. It must be a well-known person of whom everyone is likely to have heard, not someone's grandmother! The subject can only answer yes or no and you can stipulate that there should be only 20 questions, so keep score. Anyone who asks a question that has been asked before is out. The winner chooses a new person to be. It may be necessary to prepare the students with the sort of questions to ask. For example: Are you male? Are you alive? Are you European? Are you a film-star? etc.
For advanced students the radio game 'Twenty Questions' is a variation where the object can be animal, vegetable or mineral, but this game demands considerable skill and knowledge.

11. What's my nationality?

Method:
Students choose a nationality different from their own. In turn they go in front of the group and the students must guess where they come from by asking questions to which only yes or no answers are given.
Tell them to ask questions about culture, customs, geography, climate, appearance of the people, social and political systems, religion, sport, etc.
Variation:
Each student has a nationality card pinned on his or her back and they circulate, asking each other questions to find out what the nationality is. After they have guessed they try to help other students by answering questions. Make sure the students discover the nationality by means of deduction and not just wild guessing.

12. What's my occupation?

Method:
As in the previous activity either one student at a time answers questions or students have an occupation card pinned on the back.
Again you may need to give the students guidelines about the sort of questions to ask, for example:
Do you work in an office?
Do you work with your hands?
Do you work in the open air?
Do you need qualifications for this job?

Comment:
The last four games involve concentration and listening and will also help students to extend their vocabulary and increase their verbal fluency. Nos. 10 and 11 depend on students having a broad cultural knowledge.

13. Verbal boxing

Method:
In pairs students sit opposite each other and at a given signal they must start speaking on the same subject simultaneously. 'What I have done since I got up this morning', for example.
The first to run out of words or repeat herself is out. The winners then challenge each other and so on until one winner is declared.

Comment:
This is a good game for helping students to gain confidence in speaking and develop verbal fluency.

14. Merry-go-round

Method:
A and B start conversation as two characters, for example: policeman and burglar. After a short time C enters circle and completely changes the subject, addressing B in another role, for example: shop assistant. B must respond to C, no longer as a burglar but now as a customer. A sits down. Each member of the group in turn changes the subject by assuming a different role. After everyone has participated, students may come in when they like until they run out of ideas.

These conversations should be brief, just a couple of minutes each.
Variation:
Roles and situations are given on cards. Students act out in pairs – the group has to guess what the scene is about.

Comment:
This game is good preparation for role-play and forces the students 'to think on their feet'. Making an appropriate response will help the students develop concentration, listening and discourse skills. Suitable for fairly advanced students, though the teacher could prepare very simple role cards and take the game at a much slower pace for elementary students.

15. First line arguments

Method:
Students get into pairs. A is given a first line written on a piece of paper by teacher, for example:
Wife to husband: 'I'm fed up with you coming home late every night.' A says first line to B and B has to respond. The pair who produce the most heated argument are the winners.
Suggested first lines:
Customer to salesman: 'You've given me the wrong change.'
Two passengers on a train: 'You've taken my seat.'
Two neighbours: 'I've come to complain about the noise you are making.'
Two friends sharing a flat: 'I'm fed up with you leaving the washing up all the time.'
Two people in queue: 'Excuse me, I was in front of you.'
Two people in cinema: 'Would you mind keeping quiet?'

Comment:
This is a good activity for letting off steam and encouraging interaction and assertiveness. If you have any students who speak the same language, let them try it in their own language first. I did this on one occasion and later a student came to me and said 'I really needed to do that. I had been feeling very tense before the class but now I feel really relaxed after releasing all that anger.' Allowing students to have an emotional outburst within a dramatic activity can be very therapeutic.

16.   Reading the news

> **Method:**
> The student takes the role of newsreader and must improvise the reading of three news items. You can bring in newspapers and get students to select items to read. Once they have studied the pieces take the newspapers away and in turn get them to speak. They must try not to hesitate, pause or stumble – the aim is to be as articulate as possible.

Comment:
The purpose of this exercise is to help the student gain fluency and control. Suitable for advanced students.

17.   Carry-on-story

> **Method:**
> The teacher starts off a story with students sitting in a circle. Talk for about half a minute then pass it on to the next person using the link word 'and'. The last person in the circle finishes the story. For example: last night a very strange thing happened. It was about midnight. I was just getting ready for bed when there was a knock on my door. I didn't answer it immediately because I was a bit nervous *and...*

18.   One sentence story

> **Method:**
> Same as above but this time the student supplies just a single sentence in turn to form the story. Other ways of making stories would be to give the storyteller a title, a first line or a last line to use.

Comment:
Nos. 17 and 18 are good exercises in listening, concentration and discourse.

19.   Identifying objects

> **Method (i):**
> A dozen or more objects are placed on a ta ble which is set in front of the class. After ten or fifteen seconds the table is covered. The

students then write individual lists of as many of the objects as they can remember. The lists are then compared with the objects on the table.

Method (ii):
Students stand in a circle. One student is called to the centre, where he or she stands with hands behind the back. The teacher slips some object into his hands. Using his sense of touch he must guess what the object is.
Ask the student questions about the object, for example: What shape is it? Is it big or small? What's it made of?
Variation:
Teacher holds an object behind her back and asks the students to guess what it is from asking questions to which only yes or no answers can be made. For example:
Is it made of plastic?
Do you carry it around with you?
Do men use it?
Do you use it at work? etc.

Comment:
The first of these two games gives practice in observation and memorisation and can be played by elementary students. The second requires some skill in verbal questioning and is good for concentrating the mind on the sense of touch.

20. Feelings

Method (i):
Give the students a piece of paper each on which you have written the name of an emotion or state of mind, for example: jealousy, depression, frustration, anger, fear, etc.
Ask students, in pairs, to think of a situation which demonstrates the emotion. They can speak but not use the actual word on the paper.
They rehearse their scene for five minutes and return to the group to show their improvisation. The class try to guess what emotion they were acting out.

21. What am I doing?

Method:
This game should be played in exactly the same way as the previous one, but this time using verbs.
Give each pair a verb to act out or let them think of their own.
Make sure each pair is quite clear about the meaning of the verb before beginning their preparation. For example:
    to flatter, to deceive, to hinder, to flirt, to grieve, to confess, to contradict, to persuade, to exaggerate, to complain, to advise, to interfere, to cheat, to accuse.
This is a chance for students to exercise their imaginations but if any are stuck be prepared to offer ideas. For example: 'to cheat' – one of you is taking an exam. You have written some helpful information on the inside of your sleeve. You are having a peep at it when the invigilator spots you. She calls you out and asks you what you were doing.
Feed this information to the student and then let them do it in their own way.

22. What am I like?

Method:
For this game you need to prepare slips of paper with the names of adjectives describing characteristics, for example:
    proud, greedy, shy, nervous, stupid, friendly, careless, clumsy, mad, enthusiastic, conceited, bad-tempered, depressed, sad, old, happy, aggressive, sensitive.
This time the students invent a very short talk on any subject they like and try to convey by the way they deliver their speech what the characteristic is. If a student cannot think of anything to talk about find her something to read aloud.
A development could be to ask the students to get into pairs and prepare a short dialogue, using these characteristics in, say, a home setting, a work setting, meeting in the park, etc. For example: 'depressed' and 'enthusiastic' are at home together. What sort of conversation might they have?

Comment:
In the last three games the students are engaged in role-play, but, because the emphasis is on the guessing aspect of the game they will probably be less self-conscious and feel less exposed than they would if the emphasis was on how they did the role-play. As suggested earlier, games are a good

way in to role-play and give students a chance to develop gradually a more sophisticated approach. It may be necessary to prepare the students in advance for these games by making sure that the meaning of the words to be acted out are firmly understood. This might be done in their ordinary ESL class.

23. Group interview

Method:
Sit in a circle. One volunteer is the focus of the group. Anyone may ask that person any questions. He may answer honestly, or say 'I'd rather not answer that.' The purpose of the questions should be to get to know the person better – to find out what they think about different things. Continue as long as the group maintains interest.

Comment:
This is a confidence-building exercise, since the person in the middle is having to respond to a lot of people at the same time. It can be played on all levels from simple biographical questions with elementary students to questions about politics, philosophy and religion which require thought with advanced students.

24. Back to back

Method:
Students walk around the room looking at each other carefully and trying to take in as many details as possible about each other's appearance. Allow about three minutes before telling the students to stop, stand back to back with the person nearest them and in turn describe each other, for example: clothes, hair, jewelry, etc.

Comment:
This is a simple observation exercise which gives an opportunity for language practice as well.

25. Gestures

Method:
Students sit in circle. Each student makes a gesture not normally

accompanied by words, for example:

finger to lips – don't say anything

shake fist – I'm angry with you.

The others have to guess what the gesture means and find a verbal explanation for it.

Comment:

Further development of non-verbal communication. This is also a cross-cultural activity which gives students a chance to show what various gestures mean in their own cultures. It is interesting to compare the differences.

26. Famous people

Method:

Write the names of famous people on cards. Give the students a card and after making sure they know who the person is and something about them ask each one to imagine she is that person. Each student is questioned in turn to find out her identity. The difference between this and the earlier game 'Who am I?' is that this time the student should try to act as though she were that person, so she needs to think about how that person would speak, move and gesture.

When everyone has been identified the students should talk about themselves in role.

Later you could devise an improvisation with all these famous characters having a dinner party.

Comment:

This game is suitable for fairly advanced students and is a good introduction to developing character.

27. Tell us

Method:

Each student writes on a piece of paper a sentence starting 'Tell us...', for example:

Tell us about the day you arrived in England.

Tell us about your favourite place.

Tell us how you spent last weekend.

The pieces of paper go into a hat and each student in turn draws a paper and has to talk for a couple of minutes about the subject she draws.

Comment:
This game helps students to achieve verbal fluency and to think spontaneously. Talking in front of other people is a good confidence-booster as well.

28. Story-telling drama

Method:
The teacher starts to tell a story and brings the students into it to mime the actions and sometimes to speak. For example: once upon a time there was a beautiful young girl who was walking in a wood picking bluebells (pause – choose someone to be the young girl and the rest of the students to be trees – repeat the words with the students doing the actions) when suddenly she heard a strange sound behind her (choose someone to make the sound) and as she turned round with a start she saw a funny looking creature (choose the creature) ... The teacher gradually brings students into the action by pointing at them. Listening is very important as they can be brought in any time and they need to watch and listen carefully to know what has gone before. Fairy stories or other children's stories might be used for this activity.

Comment:
This is improvisation within a structure and is good preparation for work you might do later. Also involves listening skills. For advanced students.

29. Charades

Method:
Divide class into two teams and tell them to go into opposite corners of the room.
On slips of paper write song, film, book and play titles, as well as well-known sayings.
Come back to centre, sit with your team, send one person for a slip of paper from the other team. Act out the title on the paper for your own team according to the structure outlined below, while someone keeps time. After three minutes, time is up and someone from the other team gets a piece of paper and acts out.
The team tries to guess what was on the paper by concentrating on the actions of the person doing the mime.
The team with the lowest time elapsed at the end wins, so a cumulative score of minutes and seconds for each team is kept.

Structure: for acting out titles (you cannot talk):
- Show your team what the title is with agreed sign: e.g.
  movie: crank the camera
  play: pull the curtains back
  book: open hands
- Show with fingers number of words
- Show with fingers which word you are starting with
- Fingers on wrist indicate number of syllables and also which syllable, if necessary.
- Begin acting out words.
- Other signals: sounds like, little words, big words, shorten word, 'whole idea', lengthen word, etc.

Comment:
This is a useful game for concentration and communication, but it is quite sophisticated and so is only suitable with very advanced students or native speakers. A simplified version can be used with elementary students where they have to mime a compound word or a word with two or more syllables.

30.   This is your life

Method:
One person volunteers to be the director and selects an incident or event from his own life which he tells the group. The group then re-enacts the scene, under the director's supervision.
Discuss and then choose a new director.

Comment:
This is a fairly advanced activity suitable for students who have done quite a lot of drama.

7
Role-play

Role-play is a term which describes an activity widely used by educators in many different kinds of learning situations. It is a method of learning which can help people to acquire a variety of skills and insights both into themselves and into many different transactions. On management courses, for example, it is used to help students acquire management and negotiating skills. In women's groups it may be used in assertiveness training and confidence-building and in psychotherapy it can be a useful technique in helping patients to understand and come to terms wth their own mental processes and their relationship with the outside world. In drama it can be the first stage in developing character and understanding particular feelings and attitudes. Role-play can, therefore, be approached in many different ways for a variety of reasons.

In recent years role-play has become an accepted and popular method of language learning and is seen as an effective way of helping students to improve their communication skills, giving practice in using language at various levels, negotiating with other people, solving problems, making decisions, resolving situations. However, since role-play in language learning is usually seen as a way of simulating real-life situations with the student playing herself in the controlled conditions of the classroom and the teacher acting a role, I would prefer to call this method 'role-simulation' as distinct from role-play, which can have a far wider application and purpose.

In role-simulation situations are chosen that are relevant to the everyday needs and experience of the students and, by working through these situations and perhaps introducing elements of conflict or unpredictability, the student is helped to extend her powers of communication, to negotiate meaning and to present herself in an appropriate way. Part of the activity involves discussion and analysis which will help the student to discover what to say and how to say it most effectively.

Role-simulation in language learning is primarily concerned with getting the language right in terms of stress, intonation, register and effective communication in order to carry through transactions successfully.

In terms of language development and 'coping with the system', role-simulation is indeed a useful technique, but through role-play in drama one attempts to take the students much further in terms of looking beyond the words to the meaning behind them; to becoming more fully aware of different attitudes and perspectives; to understanding and projecting emotional responses to situations; to self-discovery. The role may start out as a pure stereotype, but, if the student begins to identify more completely with a personality behind the roles she moves into characterisation. To represent character is to assume a more complex personality rather than a set of attitudes alone.

Role is a pattern of behaviour prescribed by society according to a context or status which is culturally determined. For example, for a waiter to fulfil his function as a waiter successfully in this country one would probably expect him to keep some distance in the transaction. He should be friendly but not familiar, attentive but not obsequious, efficient but not fussy. Such a model waiter in another culture might be regarded as not fulfilling the role adequately at all and his behaviour might be interpreted as cold and indifferent.

To understand the subtlety of role or the behaviour and attitudes of others is not easy for the second language learner; however, if insight and understanding are the eventual aims, then true role-play, where the participants are asked to identify closely with a person or situation which may be outside their experience and to engage their imagination by trying to *feel* what it is like to be someone else, is an effective approach. To take part in imaginative role-play can be a self-revealing experience and a process which may lead to greater awareness and a modification or even a complete change of attitude and opinion, encouraging sensitivity and understanding between people. Not least it can be great fun and when you have reached the point of having fun in a second language you are well on your way to orientation in the new community.

In setting up role-play various approaches can be used, but the important factor is that the student should feel *safe*. Before embarking on role-play an atmosphere of trust in the group and confidence in the teacher must exist. The role-play might be challenging but it should never appear threatening. Students should be gently coaxed but never coerced into playing a role which they fear. One method of allaying fear of exposure that I have found quite successful is for the teacher to adopt a role in which she is vulnerable. Once you have presented yourself in an unlikely role and perhaps looked silly, students will be convinced that it's 'only acting' and that within the group there is a freedom to experiment and express themselves fully. As an early approach to role-play and improvisation many of the games described in chapter 6 offer a good starting-point.

Complaints

The following role-play situations involve making complaints and dealing with complainants. The student is faced with a confrontation situation in which the level of linguistic competence is only one factor in the transaction. She will also need the confidence to express dissatisfaction, determination to defend her position, assertiveness in the face of opposition and perhaps tact and diplomacy in dealing with a difficult or unresponsive person.[9]

Method:
Each role-play involves two, three or four people. Give out the role cards and ask the students to study them in their role-play groups, but not to look at each other's cards. They can tell each other who they are and where they are going to meet. For example:

A: 'I am a customer. I've just returned from a holiday which you arranged for me and I have some complaints about it. I am at your office.'

B: 'I am a travel agent. I arranged your holiday. I am in my office.'

Discuss when and where the holiday took place. For example: three weeks ago – Costa Brava, Spain.

In most of these role-plays the student will be taking on the role of another person, though she will obviously bring facets of her own personality to the role. Encourage her to enter imaginatively into the personality behind the role by thinking about the character she is playing and how she would expect that person to behave, for example:

What is the name, age, sex, status, family background, etc.?

It may be helpful for her to write down a brief profile.

Based on the information given on the role cards and the characters they invent the students act out their roles in turn.

Tell the students making the complaints that they should aim at a resolution to their problem if possible.

After each role-play discuss them in turn with the whole group. For example:

What sort of language was used?

Was it suitable?

Was it effective?

What manner and tone was adopted?

Was it appropriate?

Could they have achieved a better result by presenting themselves in a different way?

Which way?

Were they too mild, too emotional, too aggressive?

9. You may feel that some situations in the role-play section are not particularly relevant to your own students' lives but the emphasis is on dealing with *difficult* situations and not the particulars of the situation itself. One is concerned with expressed emotions and attitudes. However, if necessary the situations can be adapted to be more appropriate.

How did they feel in the situation?
Were they nervous, intimidated, upset, confident, angry, frustrated, etc?
Were they satisfied with the way they handled their side of the dispute?
Did they change their attitude or behaviour in response to the other person's behaviour?
If yes, why?
Make sure that all students participate in the discussion and watch each role-play carefully. The discussion is just as important as the role-play itself. Some students, because they are anxious to do their own role-play well, may be whispering to their partner about what they are going to do when they should be watching.

1. The Gas Cooker

Customer
You waited at home all day yesterday for the gas cooker you ordered to be delivered. It did not arrive. You have taken time off from work for which you will lose your pay to await the delivery. You go to the gas company the next day in your lunch hour to complain. If you do not get satisfaction from the clerk you may ask to see the manager. You want compensation for the time lost and a guarantee that the cooker will be delivered promptly.

Clerk
In your job you are listening to complaints all day. You are bored with them and it is almost time for your lunch hour to begin. You are very hungry. You check the paperwork and it appears that the cooker went out yesterday but the men couldn't get any answer from the house. The customer insists she was in all day so you check the address – the house number is wrong. Did the customer give the wrong number or was it taken down incorrectly when the order was made in the showroom?

Manager
You are new in this job and fairly enthusiastic. You have the authority to give compensation if the customer has a genuine grievance but you must consider the facts carefully first. If you think the customer did not give her address correctly then it is not your responsibility.

2. The Telephone Bill

Customer
You have received a telephone bill for £300. You know it must be wrong. Usually your bill is about £30 a month and you have not made any

additional calls. You go to the telephone company to dispute it.

Clerk

You are usually polite to customers but today you are in a particularly bad mood and this is the third complaint you've had this morning. Telephone bills are computerized and you argue that they cannot be wrong. You tell the customer that if she refuses to pay, her 'phone may be disconnected. You are not sympathetic at all.

---

3. The Hospital

Patient

You have gone to the casualty department of a hospital because you are ill or you've had an accident. You've been waiting nearly two hours and people who came after you have been seen. You go to reception to complain.

Receptionist

In your job you are dealing with the public all day and some of them are very difficult. You consider this patient's problem is minor compared with some of the cases coming in. As far as you are concerned the people who make most fuss are not usually very ill.

---

4. The Restaurant

Customer

You have just had a meal in a very expensive restaurant. The food was bad but you ate most of it. The service was terrible. When the bill comes you think it is too much so you call the waiter to complain about the bill, the quality of the food and the service. You also want to impress your companion with the idea that nobody gets the better of you.

Companion

You were invited to dinner by A who is now making a fuss. You agree that the food and service were not very good but you hate scenes and you feel embarrassed. You try to stop him from complaining. You feel everyone in the restaurant is looking at you. You would rather pay the bill and leave.

Waiter

You are new in the job and very inexperienced. You don't speak English very well. You don't think the food is very good but you dare not say so. You are worried that if this customer complains about you you will get the sack. You are not in a position to change the bill.

Manager

Your restaurant is going through a bad phase. You are having difficulty finding good staff and recently you employed a new cook who is not very good. It is the policy of the restaurant to change food if it is not eaten but not to give reductions on the bill. You must decide how to handle this difficult customer who is attracting a lot of attention.

5. The Travel Agent

Customer
You have just returned from a holiday abroad. The accommodation was very bad and the food was terrible. The hotel was miles from the beach and your room looked out onto the sewer. You are very angry and you go to the travel agents who arranged the holiday to complain.

Travel Agent
Your business has a 'get-rich-quick' philosophy and you are not too concerned about your reputation. You will always try to fob people off with excuses if you can. It depends how well they seem to know their rights as to whether you would offer compensation or not.

6. The Dentist

Customer
You made an appointment over the telephone to see your dentist. When you arrive the receptionist says that you have come on the wrong day. She has no record of the appointment on that day but finds it entered in the book for the following week. You are quite sure you have got the day right and you have taken time off from work.

Receptionist
You made this appointment over the phone. You pride yourself on your efficiency and you hardly ever make a mistake. You are quite sure the patient has got the date wrong. You are not prepared to admit that the error could be yours. The dentist is fully booked so it would be very difficult to fit her in today.

7. The College

Student
You joined a class (choose your own subject) at a college and paid a lot of money for the course. You are very dissatisfied with the quality of teaching and the teacher is often late and doesn't give you any attention. You go to the Principal to ask for your money back.

Principal
You listen to the student's complaints but the college has a policy of not

refunding fees once they've been collected. The teacher in question has been at the college for many years and you doubt whether you can do much if the complaints are well-founded.

8. The Office

Typist
You have recently taken a job as a typist but since you started you have not been asked to do any typing. The supervisor asks you to make tea, run personal errands, do filing, etc. You go to see the boss to complain.

Boss
You are fairly new in this job. You don't know much about what goes on in the outer office but you find the supervisor of the typing pool rather overbearing. She has worked there for many years and thinks she owns the place. You want a quiet life but you don't like to see people being exploited so you must take the complaints to the supervisor if you feel they are genuine.

Supervisor
You have worked for this company for many years and you have seen bosses come and go. You feel you have the right to use the new girl in any way you choose. You do not take kindly to criticism. You are angry when you discover this girl has been complaining and insist that she should be sacked.

9. Good Neighbours

Neighbour (A)
You discover that your next-door neighbour is building an extension to the kitchen which will completely block out your light. Work is already in progress. You have never been on very friendly terms. You go to her house to complain.

Neighbour (B)
You are building an extension to your kitchen. You do not believe it will affect your next-door neighbour so you didn't tell her. You don't care for her anyway.

10. Social Services

Client
You go to the DHSS office to complain that your Giro hasn't arrived. You are unemployed and you have no other source of income. You 'phoned yesterday and they said it was in the post. Tomorrow is Saturday and you have no money for the weekend.

Clerk
You are dealing with complainants all day and you are very tired and overworked. You check and the Giro is in the post so the fault is with the post office. You have to decide whether to issue another cheque and cancel the first or tell the client she will have to wait.

---

11. Second-Hand Cars

Customer
You have just bought a second-hand car from someone who advertised it in the local paper. When you get it home you discover some serious faults. You paid £500. You go back to the owner to complain.

Car Owner
As far as you are concerned the car was all right when you sold it. You think it was worth £500. You have already spent the money so you can't give them a refund even if you wanted to.

---

12. The Dry Cleaners

Customer
You have just collected a very expensive silk dress from the dry cleaner's. It has stains on it that were not there before and it has shrunk. You go back to the shop to complain.

Shop Assistant
Dry cleaning is a risky business and there is a notice in the shop saying that the shop is not responsible for any shrinkage. As far as the stains are concerned you argue that they must have been there before. You very rarely give compensation.

---

13. Pets

Neighbour (A)
You have gone to your next-door neighbour to complain about their dog who keeps getting into your garden, making messes and ruining your plants. There is a hole in the fence on your neighbour's side and it is her responsibility to repair it.

Neighbour (B)
You are an old lady living alone. Your dog is your only companion and you are devoted to him. You know there is a hole but you can't afford to have it repaired. You think your neighbour is making a fuss about nothing.

14. The Worker

Boss

You are a boss who is very dissatisfied with the work of one of your employees. He is lazy and often late or absent. You would like to sack him but he is protected by the employment act. You call him into your office for a talk.

Employee

You don't work very hard because you think you are very badly paid. You don't like the work – it is boring and monotonous. You would like something more challenging to do. Often you come late or stay home because your are depressed.

---

15. Noisy Neighbours

Neighbour (A)

You have new neighbours who are making your life a misery with their constant shouting and playing of loud music. You call on them to complain.

Neighbour (B)

You are just living the way you always have. You think your neighbour is prejudiced against you because you come from another country and your skin is a different colour.

---

16. The Rent

Tenant

Your landlord has just informed you by letter that he is increasing your rent by 50 per cent. He never does any repairs or improvements and you think he is exploiting you. You go to see him.

Landlord

You think the previous rent was far too low. You do not like this tenant. The family live in the flat above you and they cook strange-smelling foreign food and have lots of visitors. You would like them to leave and you hope by putting up the rent they may decide to move.

N.B. In the last two role-plays I have included the theme of racism. It is, unfortunately, a part of life and an issue that needs to be faced. Whether a teacher introduces this theme into the drama lesson in role-play or improvisation must be a matter of personal choice and judgement, but I have found it a subject that students are eager to confront and discuss. Most students will have a personal experience to describe that involves racial discrimination or racial hatred and it may be possible to devise role-plays which will exploit the students' own experience and help them to find ways to cope with it.

Comment:
The role-plays are concerned with self-presentation in difficult situations and the main aim should be to help the students find the best way to express themselves and achieve the desired result. This will be through the manner in which they approach the situation and the language they use. Confrontation can be very unpleasant, but in the real world it is something we all have to face from time to time, and role-play can be a useful method of finding the most effective way to handle a difficult situation. Cultural differences may produce different approaches and these need to be looked at and discussed. Does a forceful and domineering approach, for example, which may work in some places, work here? Can bribery be used? Is an obsequious approach likely to get results? The role-plays need to be seen in their cultural context.

When analysing the effect of the role-play with students you may wish to correct any gross grammatical errors, but the main emphasis should be placed on the presentation and the interaction that occurs, as the language used is only one element of the total experience. To assist the discussion the teacher and the students can make notes which the role-play is in progress or it can be tape- or video-recorded if the facilities are available and the students feel comfortable working with video. A video-recording will greatly aid any discussion on the para-linguistic aspect of the work.

A useful follow-up to some of these role-play situations would be to consider one's rights and responsibilities, since, where they cannot be settled amicably, recourse to legal action may be necessary and students should know where they can get advice.

Bad news
The following role-plays involve the imparting of bad news. This is another transaction which inevitably causes some degree of shock or distress but we may sometimes soften the blow by choosing our words carefully and handling the situation with sensitivity. We may wish to minimise the pain our news will inflict or we may be trying to find a way of minimising our own responsibility or guilt for what has occurred. Depending on the situation and the persons involved we must decide which approach is the most appropriate. Should we use tact and diplomacy or is a direct, honest approach to be favoured?

Method:
Follow the same procedure suggested for the 'Complaints' role-plays. Give the cards and ask the students to study their roles and invent a character for themselves, discussing only who they are and where the situation takes place with their role-play partner. Take each role-play in turn to discuss with the whole group and consider whether the language and the behaviour was appropriate for each particular situation.

1. Flat Sharing

Flat-sharer (A)
For the past six months you have shared your flat with someone, partly for company and partly to help with the rent, but you are not very happy with this person. Her habits and ways of living are not compatible with yours. You are a non-smoker and a vegetarian, you like classical music, you are very tidy and lead a quiet life. Your flat-mate smokes, drinks, eats meat, plays jazz, is untidy and has noisy parties. You hate confrontations but you feel you must tell her to find somewhere else to live.

Flat-sharer (B)
You are sharing A's flat. You do not have much in common. You smoke and drink, she doesn't. You like jazz, she likes classical music. You like parties and having friends in, she doesn't. However, it's a lovely flat and it would be difficult for you to find anything as good so you are prepared to put up with your differences.

2. Problems with Mother

Husband and Wife
Your widowed mother lives with you. She is always complaining and criticising everything you both do. She is ruining your lives and causing constant arguments in the home. You plan to move and you don't want her to go with you. She has enough money to buy a small flat for herself. You must break the news.

Mother
Your husband died two years ago and you have lived with your son and his wife ever since. You disapprove of the way they live but they never listen to your advice. You think it is their duty to provide you with a home and you would hate to live alone.

3. It's a Dog's Life

Neighbour (A)
You have just run over and killed your neighbour's dog who ran out into the road as you were passing in your car. You tried to stop but it was too late. You go to your neighbour to break the news.

Neighbour (B)
You are an elderly person living alone but you have a wonderful dog as a companion. He has been with you for ten years and you are devoted to him. You don't go out much because you have a bad leg but your dog runs about in the garden.

4. We Want Your House

Council worker
You are an employee from the council. You have called on X to inform her that her house is going to be compulsorily purchased by the council for a road-widening scheme. The council will buy the house and then knock it down. The owner will have to move within two months.

House owner
You are an elderly person living alone with your two cats. You live in a lovely cottage which has been in your family for three generations. You are very attached to your home and look forward to spending the rest of your life there.

5. The Car

Friend (A)
This afternoon you borrowed your friend's car without permission and damaged it in an accident. You know she is planning to drive to Spain tomorrow for a holiday. You will have to break the news.

Friend (B)
Tomorrow you are going to drive your car to Spain for a holiday. You are very excited. You are at home now busy packing. Your best friend calls on you.

6. Arrest

Policeman
You are a policeman. You call on X to tell her that her son/daughter has been arrested for shop-lifting. The child is 14 years old.

Mother
You have a teenage son/daughter who is quite a worry to you. You are a

one-parent family and you have to go out to work. You are afraid that your child has too much freedom and may get into trouble one day.

7. Burglary

Neighbour (A)
Your next-door neighbour's house was burgled while they were away on holiday. You are waiting for them as they arrive back to give them the bad news.

Neighbour (B)
You have been away on holiday for two weeks and you are just returning home. You have a nice house which you are looking forward to getting back to.

8. Marriage

Husband or Wife
You have been married for ten years. You haven't any children. Your marriage is not a happy one. For some time now you have been seeing someone else who wants you to marry him/her. You want a divorce. You must break the news.

Husband or Wife
You have been married for ten years. You haven't any children. Your marriage is not a happy one. You feel your husband/wife neglects you. You have tried hard to make the marriage work and you do not want him/her to leave you.

9. The Business

Employer
You run a small family business which is doing badly. You have three employees but in order to survive you will have to reduce your staff. You decide to make the last person to join the firm redundant. You call him/her in.

Employee
You work for a small family business. You have had this job for one year. You like the work very much and you need to keep your job as you have a large family to support. You work much harder than the other two employees but they have been with the firm for many years.

Comment:
As with 'Complaints' we are concerned here with self-presentation in difficult situations and what sort of manner and approach is the most appropriate. We are also concerned with examining our emotional responses. How do we feel when we receive bad news and how do we handle our feelings? Though the students are projecting themselves into fictitious situations and are assuming attitudes which are not necessarily their own, they are, in the process, exploring their own emotions and gaining insight into other people's. They are also getting practice in coping with new situations.

Spontaneous role-play

The following role-play situations aim to give students practice in interpreting the meaning behind language and behaviour and responding appropriately. They will need to 'think on their feet'; deduce what is going on and respond accordingly; use their imaginations; develop the ability to *ad lib*; and interpret a situation by reading the signals.

In life, language comes at us from all directions, often in a kind of shorthand or code which we must decipher. The context is not always clear. For example:

A stranger comes up to you in the street:

'Excuse me, have you got 10p please?'

Is this a down-and-out asking for 10p for a cup of tea or is it someone requiring change for the telephone? If they are standing next to the telephone box it is probably the latter but if not how do we interpret the request? Appearances often present us with clues but not always, so we look at the accompanying behaviour, that is, a tramp will probably be holding a hand out and may adopt an obsequious posture; a telephone caller will probably be showing you some coins they want to change and will make the utterance in a polite and matter-of-fact tone. Sometimes we enter a conversation or situation when it is already in progress but we pick up clues from what is being said about what has gone before and we catch the mood from the tone of voice and the non-verbal behaviour.

In these role-play situations only student A knows what it is about; student B, therefore, must interpret and respond.

Method:
Ask students to find a partner. Give role card to A and ask her to study it for a few minutes. A and B then go in front of the class and A starts to act out her role, directing her words at B who must respond by accepting the role A imposes on her. The rest of the group watching are in the position of B, so they too will be interpreting, but passively.

Example:
You are a customs official. You want to check the luggage of B
who is passing through the 'Nothing to Declare' hall.
A: Over here please. Put your suitcase on the counter.
B: (lifts case up)
A: Is it locked?
B: Yes.
A: Please unlock it.
B: (unlocks case)
A: (starts checking the contents) Where did you get this gold
watch, sir?
B: In Zurich.
A: Would you please show me the receipt.
B: I've lost it.
A: Oh, that's very unfortunate for you, sir. (etc.)

Spontaneous role-play situations

1
You are a store detective. You have just apprehended a customer you
suspect of shoplifting.

2
You are at the police station. You have gone there to report that your
husband/wife is missing. You haven't seen him/her for two days.

3
You are a hypnotist. You are trying to help a client who wants to give up
smoking.

4
You are a salesman trying to persuade a housewife to buy a vacuum
cleaner. You give a demonstration.

5
You are asking your boss if you can have a day off from work next week.
Think of a good excuse.

6
You are a policeman. You have just stopped someone you have seen
climbing out of a window. You ask for an explanation.

80

7

You are asking an employee for an explanation for his absence from work yesterday.

8

You are a policeman questioning a witness who saw a car accident or robbery.

9

You are a psychoanalyst. You are talking to a patient who claims to hear voices.

10

You are a wife whose husband has just come home. It's midnight and you expected him at 6 p.m. You are asking him for an explanation. You suspect he has been out with another woman.

11

You are a driving instructor. The person you are teaching is driving very badly and doesn't seem to understand the controls although you have explained a dozen times. You are impatient.

12

You have just found out that your best friend has been seeing your boyfriend behind your back. You confront her.

13

You have been waiting outside a telephone box to make a call for twenty minutes. You knock on the door and ask the person inside to hurry up.

14

You are on a long-distance train. You have a reserved seat. You leave your seat to go to the bar and when you return someone is sitting there. You confront them.

15

You are selling your car. You are showing it to a prospective buyer. Take him out in it to show how it runs.

16

You have gone to look at a house you are interesting in buying. The estate agent arranged an appointment. Ask the owner to show you round. Make an offer.

17

You have advertised for someone to share your flat. You are interviewing a prospective tenant. You want a compatible tenant so find out all you can about him/her.

18

You are visiting your child's teacher. You are not satisfied with her progress and you suspect the teacher is not doing her job properly. She never brings any homework from school.

19

You are a policeman. You have asked a motorist to stop. You suspect he has been drinking as he was speeding and going off the road. You take his details and give him a breath test.

20

You are a doctor seeing a patient. The patient complains of stomach pains. You suspect appendicitis and arrange for her to go into hospital immediately.

Comment:

These role-plays are only suitable for fairly advanced students. Although most of the situations are simple enough it takes some degree of linguistic skill to pick up the clues and enter spontaneously a conversation for which there was no preparation in terms of defining the role or the situation. The instructions for the role-plays are intentionally brief in order to give students A the maximum opportunity to exercise their imagination and define their own role within the situation. If they are playing the role of the policeman, for example, they can decide what kind of policeman they will be. Once the role-play is under way students A will have to use their wits just as much as B; although they are the initiators they will have to respond to the answers they get from B which may not be what they expect.

How would the student playing the role of psychoanalyst resolve his situation, for instance? He would need to offer some sort of advice or treatment. When I did this particular role-play with some post-elementary ESL students, I was impressed with the 'while you wait' diagnosis that emerged. The student playing the role of patient said the voices were cries for help – she didn't know whose voice it was but it always said: 'Help me, help me, please help me.' The 'analyst', after some probing, concluded that the woman was sadly neglected by her husband, had no family and longed to be needed; thus she had invented the voices to compensate for her need to be needed!

Imaginative role-play

Continuing the theme of interpreting the meaning behind language and behaviour, these role-plays are based on 'first lines' and the students have to invent their own roles and situations accordingly.

Method:

Ask the students to work in pairs. Give student A a 'first line' written on a piece of paper and ask her to invent a context where she might say the line to B.

After a few minutes thinking time each pair go out in front and A delivers the first line; for example:

A: *'What on earth are you doing out of bed?'*

A might have thought she was a nurse talking to a patient. B might have thought she was a child and A was the mother checking up on her. If B has interpreted the situations differently then A must adapt her role accordingly, as follows:

A: What on earth are you doing out of bed?

B: I'm looking for my drawing-book.

A: Get back into bed at once. You should be asleep.

B: I'm not tired.

A: Get back into bed and I'll read you a story.

First lines

1. Where on earth have you been?
2. I'm sorry but I really must go.
3. Look, would you please leave me alone?
4. Would you please go back to your seat and wait like everyone else?
5. I'm afraid that anything you say may be taken down and used in evidence against you.
6. How long have you had this pain?
7. Whatever are you doing here?
8. How did you get in?
9. I'm afraid you have failed.
10. Don't panic – someone must come soon.

11. Excuse me, could you take me across the road please?
12. Please calm down and tell me exactly what you saw.
13. Why don't you get off your backside and give me a hand?
14. How long do you wish to stay in this country?
15. I gave you a five pound note!
16. Can't you see that notice?
17. I'm sorry but you are too late.
18. It was your fault entirely.
19. Stand up and put your hands on your head.
20. I was before you.

Comment:
If you give each pair the same 'first line' there will be a lot of scope for discussing similarities and differences or alternative situations. For example, language is appropriate on many occasions, but intonation etc. will alter the meaning.

Interviews
The following role-plays are based on interview situations of various kinds, formal, informal and public. They will give the students an opportunity to improve their question-and-answer technique; to use language appropriately; to work on self-presentation and building confidence.

1. FORMAL – Interviews for employment
To be successful in a job interview does not depend on experience and qualifications alone. Preparation is essential and the manner in which you present yourself, exploit your own qualities or disguise your deficiencies is equally important. Confidence and self-esteem are the keys and role-play can help to develop these qualities.

Method:
Ask the students to think of a job they would like to apply for that would match their own experience or qualifications or, if they haven't any, to invent a job and invent appropriate skills. The group then work out some job descriptions, one for each person, or you can take them from newspapers. For example:

West End Store requires a typist to work in their despatch department. Must have good speeds and previous experience. Hours 9–5. Five-day week. Three weeks holiday p.a. Pension Scheme, canteen. Salary £4,000 p.a.

Give the students an application form to complete:

Name . . . . Address . . . .

Age: . . . . Status: . . . .

Details of Eduction . . . .

. . . .

Qualifications . . . .

Previous Employment . . . .

Interests . . . .

Names and addresses of two referees . . . .

. . . .

When the students have completed their application forms ask them to get into pairs. A will play the part of the interviewer and B the applicant. Together they should study the job description and the application form.

Discuss in the group the type of questions the interviewer should ask and how the interview should be conducted. How long should it last? How can the application form be used to find out more about the candidate?

Next set up each interview in turn and ask the rest of the group to observe and make notes. Ask them to consider how the applicant presents herself. How does she walk into the room, sit down, begin the interview, etc.?

Is she confident and composed or nervous and fidgity?

Does she look at her feet or at the interviewer?

Where are her hands?

Does she smile or look miserable?

Does she speak clearly or is she barely audible?

Then consider the questions and the manner in which she answers them.

Is she hesitant and unsure of her answers or does she know exactly what she wants to say?

Does she do herself justice or is she too modest and self-effacing?

Does she expand her answers to her advantage or just give yes and no answers?

Does she show any initiative in the interview by leading the questioner to ask the questions she wants to answer?

Does she appear to be enthusiastic or dull?

It might be useful to give the observers a check-list to study before embarking on the interviews.

After each role-play discuss these questions fully and perhaps re-run bits of the interview that could be improved.

Comment:

It should be emphasised that the role-plays provide the raw material to work on and that the discussion and analysis are of prime importance. Similar role-plays could be devised to deal with applying for courses in colleges, training schemes etc., where self-presentation is also important.

2. Informal interviews

There are occasions when the purpose of an interview is simply to find out what sort of person you are. The interviewer is most interested in your personality and personal outlook on life. These informal interviews will give students an opportunity to express their own personalities or they might like to treat them as imaginative exercises and invent a personality to fit the situation.

(a) Flat-sharing

Method:
Present students with the following advertisement (or something similar).

'Two professional young men and female nurse require 4th person similar to share house. Prefer female. Own room, share duties, Hendon area. £30 p.w. + shared bills.'

Choose three students to play the above roles. Ask them to get together and discuss what sort of person they are looking for who will be compatible with their life style. They must invent personalities for themselves and discuss how they live in this house and what are their likes and dislikes, etc.

Next ask the other students to imagine they have answered this advertisement and they are going to be seen in turn by the three occupants. Both parties have got to try to get to know each other to see if they would be compatible.

Get the whole group to think about the sort of questions that might be asked in order to find out whether the applicant is suitable.

Is he/she sociable or unsociable? Quiet, introverted or noisy and extroverted? Reliable or unreliable? Would he/she share the housework? Does the applicant have any unacceptable habits, for example, smoking, drinking, etc? Does he/she have many friends? Is he/she looking for companions or just somewhere to live?

When each person has been interviewed ask the three to decide whom they want to choose and ask the others if they had wanted to be chosen.

Comment:
This role-play exercise would be suitable for post-elementary students. A variation would be to organise the interviews in pairs. Ask A to be the flat owner and B to be the applicant. They can then make up their own advertisements.

(b)   Marriage bureau or dating agency

> Method:
> Prepare an application form for the students to complete.
> Name:
> Address:
> Age:
> Occupation:
> Education:
> Interests:
> Ask the students to complete these forms with an invented character in mind.
> In pairs A plays interviewer and B client. A asks B questions based on the application form and B describes the sort of person they would like to meet for friendship or marriage.
> They practise in pairs and then each pair shows their interview to the group.
> Then swap roles.

Comment:
This is a fun activity and gives students an opportunity to be inventive. Don't ask students to play themselves in this situation unless they really want to. It could be embarrassing. A follow-up activity could be the first meetings of a couple arranged by the bureau.

3.   Television interviews
These are public interviews where the person being interviewed must be conscious not only of the interviewer but of the audience so considerable poise and confidence are needed. The interviews can take place with the rest of the class representing an invited audience on television so that they can also have an opportunity of asking questions. The job of the interviewer will be to conduct the interview and programme, that is, introduce the guest, ask questions, bring in the audience, conclude.

> Method:
> Prepare role cards about famous or interesting people, or imaginary people in the news. Give a description of the person

and some biographical details, for example:

> Your name is Jenny Myers. You are 25. You have just become London's first woman taxi driver. Your father was a taxi driver and it has always been your ambition to be one but traditionally it has been a man's job. In spite of great opposition and hostility you have finally succeeded and today you have had your first experience of working as a London cabbie.

Give a copy of the role card to the interviewer and the interviewee and give them five minutes together to prepare the interview. They show it to the group and later on the interviewer invites the audience to ask questions.

Suggestions for role-cards
1. Kidnapped heiress who has just been released after six months of being held hostage.
2. Winner of £100,000 football pool ten years ago – now penniless. What happened to the money?
3. Famous actor and actress about to marry each other again for the third time. Each has also been married to two other people and divorced.
4. Founder of new religious cult which is being highly criticised. Its headquarters is a large country mansion. Parents are very worried about their children who have joined this secret order.
5. Young person who is leading a protest movement against unemployment and has gone on hunger strike.
6. Person who claims to be in spiritual contact with various well-known people who are now deceased.
7. You have just won the 'Mastermind' competition on television. You left school at 15 and have worked in a shop ever since. You come from a poor family and everyone is surprised at your great achievement.
8. You were an employee at a car factory. You have just been sacked for refusing to join a union which is compulsory for all employees.

Taken from life
This time the students create their own characters but they are based on real people that are well known to everyone. In pairs they prepare an interview with appropriate questions and answers. The group must watch each interview and try to guess the identity of the personality from the questions and answers given. Choose from actors, actresses, politicians, artists, musicians, sportsmen or women, people in the public eye, etc.

8
Improvisation

In essence improvisation is a play without a script. Because there is no script, an improvised play does not depend on any skill or ability at reading, or of remembering lines, and is, therefore, an activity that students of varying levels of literacy competence are able to participate in and enjoy.

It utilises points shown on the figure below, and depends on the full use of each person's own resources.

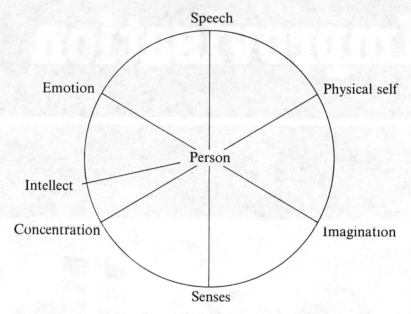

Taken from *Development through Drama,* Brian Way

Improvisation is a group activity in which students create people and relationships in time and place, and act out a situation using speech and movement, but usually without any preconceived plan. It is a process, not a performance, and the emphasis is on thoughts, feelings, and language which arise out of it.

Basically there are two kinds of improvisation: 'spontaneous improvisation' which is an open-ended process usually initiated by the teacher, and 'prepared improvisation' in which the group works towards a finished dramatic statement. In 'spontaneous improvisation' as in 'spontaneous role-play' the aim is to help the students to discover the meaning behind language and behaviour. The students are presented with a situation and are faced with the challenge to respond and interact in a way which is appropriate. The teacher, acting as a sort of catalyst, will introduce a situation and try to create a drama in which the students can suspend their disbelief and become involved. The great advantage of this approach with students who may be relatively new to drama is that they can be in the drama but playing a passive role. No one is forced to become actively involved before they feel ready to participate.

Spontaneous improvisation

Approach 1

Method:
The class sit in a circle. The teacher emphasises that the play takes place only in the circle. If she or anyone leaves the circle they are out of the play.
(*Subject: A residents' meeting on a housing estate.*)
The students are not told what the subject is. The teacher simply comes into the circle and sits down.
Teacher: Good evening, ladies and gentlemen. We have three main items on our agenda tonight. They are (1) dustbins; (2) the 50% increase in our service charge and (3) the problem of pets on the estate. If anyone would like to include any other matter they can bring it up under 'any other business'.
Now Mr Smith, our secretary is ill so could I have a volunteer to take the minutes, please?
(Hopefully a student will volunteer and she is then handed a notebook and pen to take down the minutes.)
Right. I understand that there have been lots of complaints from residents recently that the dustbins are not being emptied. Would anyone like to say something about this?
(By now the students should be tuned-in to the situation and will begin to participate. The teacher's role will be to lead the discussion and stimulate a response.)
If you have a particularly reticent group it may be a good idea to alert one member of the group before you start and get them to make provocative remarks.

Further suggestions for spontaneous improvisation
- Shop stewart calls out workers on a factory shop floor.
- Group interview for a mysterious and dangerous mission abroad. People have responded to a newspaper advertisement asking for volunteers.
- Survivors of a plane crash or shipwreck cast ashore on a desert island.
- Hostages.
- Women in prison contemplating a riot as a protest against conditions.
- A group of illegal immigrants awaiting deportation.

- A parents' meeting in a school to discuss drug abuse.
- A public meeting to discuss a proposed by-pass which would cut through a village.
- A group of people who are meeting to discuss setting up a commune which would be self-supporting and run on communistic lines.
- A group of people being interviewed who claim to have had paranormal experiences.
- A group of single-parent families discussing their problems.
- A group of people who want to start a new political party.

Approach 2

Method:

Name a situation, for example, 'A street market'. Give each student a role card and then allow them to get on with it. The drama will be structured only to the extent that you will feed people into the scene gradually.

First choose two or three people to be stall-holders and ask them to go and set up their stalls.

Secondly, choose the shoppers and ask them to make shopping lists. Most of the shoppers will be ordinary people but on the card they may have something specific to do.

Here is a list of examples. Choose one or two people who will be asked to do something that will create a dramatic tension in the situation and give the others something specific to respond to.

- shopper with dog on a leash
- shopper – very elderly lady
- shopper – can't speak much English
- shoppers – newly married couple shopping together for the first time
- shopper – the stallholder has given you the wrong change
- shopper – becomes ill and fall down in the street
- shopper – shopping is a pretext for looking for something to steal – a purse for example
- illegal seller with suitcase
- policeman.

Make sure all the students know who the stall-holders are and what they are selling and identify the policeman in case he may be needed, but do not reveal the other roles. Allow them to emerge as the street scene develops and the students begin to interact.

Do not include more than one or two characters who will create a disturbance. If you do the result will be utter chaos.

Further suggestions for spontaneous improvisation
- A casualty department of a hospital
- An employment agency
- An airport lounge
- A customs hall
- A department store
- A factory
- A hotel lobby
- A school or college
- A doctor's waiting room
- A train
- A police station
- A pub
- A party
- A desert island

Comment:
Through spontaneous improvisation students gain practice in language and communication skills and they develop their emotional range by playing roles that may be unfamiliar to them and outside their own experience.

The spontaneous improvisation also presents students with the need to negotiate, co-operate, solve problems and make decisions.

Prepared improvisation

In a prepared improvisation the group is, in effect, making up a play, so there will be some attention to form. The play should have a beginning, a middle and an end. Starting with a basic theme or situation, during the process of the improvisation the group will develop their ideas, select and shape them and organise them into a structure which will be communicable to others.

After choosing a theme there should be discussion of the implications of the theme, preparation in small groups and finally a presentation to the whole group when the small groups are satisfied with their 'play'. This sort of group-prepared improvisation will give the students practice in working together and sharing ideas and decision-making. It will also help them to develop language that is suitable to the subject and to express themselves coherently.

Method:
Theme: 'Greed'
Situation: A solicitor's office and waiting-room.

Divide the class into groups of five.

Tell them to choose one person to be the solicitor.

The others have been named to appear to hear the last will and testament of Sir Rupert Featherstone, a wealthy industrialist who has recently died. They must each decide who they want to be, for example: wife, son or daughter, friend; a mystery person, e.g. mistress, illegitimate son or daughter, chauffeur, etc. The students discuss the situation and then they act out their roles, first in the waiting-room of the solicitor's office as they anticipate what each has been left and then in the office when the solicitor reads the will. The student playing the solicitor will have a free hand in deciding who has been left what. At this stage there may be some strong emotional responses to what they hear. Are they satisfied? Is the will fair? Do any of them wish to contest the will?

A useful dramatic device which the teacher can use to elicit information and/or a response from a student is to 'freeze' the drama, that is, tell everyone to hold their pose and then to question any of the participants about themselves and how they felt. For example:

Teacher:	You are Featherstone's wife, aren't you?
Student:	Yes, I am.
Teacher:	How long were you married?
Student:	Twenty years.
Teacher:	Was it a happy marriage?
Student:	Yes, very happy.
Teacher:	Did you know that your husband had a mistress?
Student:	No, I certainly didn't.
Teacher:	How do you feel about that?
Student:	I'm very upset and shocked. I can't believe it.
Teacher:	What do you think about his leaving her so much money?
Student:	It's wrong. She has no right. He must have been sick in his mind when he made this will.
Teacher:	(*to mistress*) Was Sir Rupert happily married?
Student:	No, he hated his family.
Teacher:	Why?
Student:	They were so selfish. They only cared about his money. They did nothing for him, especially his wife. He couldn't talk to her.

Of course this technique does interrupt the spontaneous flow of the drama but it can be used effectively in terms of clarification, and for heightening the dramatic tension of the situation.

94

Further suggestions for prepared improvisation
1. Four or five people working together in an office. They have been told that one of them is about to be made redundant and they discuss who it is likely to be.
2. Four or five people working together in an office. They have been told that one of them is to be promoted to the position of the boss's personal secretary. They discuss who it is likely to be and why.
3. Four people unknown to each other waiting on an empty platform of a country railway station. It is past midnight and they are waiting for a train. There is an announcement that the train has been cancelled and there will not be another one until tomorrow. They must decide what to do. There is a waiting-room but it has no heating.
5. A number of women who have just been sent to prison. They have just met and will be sharing a dormitory. They discuss who they are and what they have done.
6. A reunion of old school friends. They have not met for ten years. They discuss what has happened to them over the years.
7. A group of people who are guests at a hotel where there has been a murder. One plays the role of police detective and questions the guests in turn.
8. A group has survived a plane crash on an unknown island. The natives discover them. They are friendly but they don't speak the same language.
9. A group of survivors of a nuclear holocaust. They must decide how to build a new community.
10. A jury. A murder trial has just finished and they must decide whether the accused is guilty or not guilty. (They will need first to invent the crime and the evidence they have been presented with.)

Comment:
Prepared improvisation gives the students the opportunity to discuss their ideas and to plan and organise a dramatic statement.

Working together on a group project helps students to build relationships with each other and develop mutual support.

9
Making a play

In this chapter I will describe the process of making a play. Several scripts are included which are the result of work done with students and which are suitable for advanced ESL/EFL students or native speakers.

Playmaking uses the students own ideas and language following an initial stimulus from the teacher and does not necessarily imply presentation before an audience. It involves devoting a number of lessons to the project so that it can be developed into a piece of work of some substance and with a certain attention to detail. It also enables the class to look at narrative and dramatic structure in a critical way.

Although there are some plays that have been specially written for learners of English I have not found any that students either particularly liked or found interesting or relevant to their lives. It was for this reason that I decided to write some scripts with students based on themes they had already explored and using their own language as far as possible.

Making a play involves commitment on the part of the students, as the play develops through a sequence of lessons and everyone has a part to play. I found students were in fact very conscientious about their attendance during this period as they realised that an absent member of the team could upset the progress of the work. It is essential that the whole group are present from the beginning to the end. If it is not feasible to depend on this sort of commitment from your students then it is probably better to confine the drama lesson to work that can be completed in only one or two lessons.

A group drama project

This is a project for post-elementary ESL/EFL students or native speakers who already have some drama experience. The project will probably take at least six two-hour sessions to complete.

Method

1. *Choose a situation* which will lend itself to dramatic interpretation and involve a lot of interaction with the students, for example:
    The casualty department of a London hospital late on a Saturday night.
2. *Set the scene:* describe and discuss the casualty department – how it functions, who are the staff, who are the patients, why they go there, the procedures, the atmosphere, etc. Ask students to relate any experiences they have had of 'casualty' either here or in their own country.
3. *Allocate roles:* roles may be devised by the teacher and typed on cards (see 101) or, if the students feel sufficiently confident, they can devise their own. In this case, the doctor, the nurse and the receptionist are key roles and they should be discussed by the group

before starting as everyone needs to know who they are and to have a clear idea of their function in the play.

The other roles should not be discussed in the group at this stage. The students can play their roles according to the description they have received on their role cards without prior knowledge of the other roles. This way they will be encouraged to react to and interact with the other actors as they appear to each other.

The acting-out of the situation in the first instance will therefore be more naturalistic and spontaneous. The students play their part, but they must also be aware of and listen to their colleagues to find out who they are and how to relate to them.

4. *Role preparation:* before starting the improvisation, ask students to study their roles in order that they can begin to identify more completely with the personalities behind the roles and move towards characterisation, which is to assume a more complex personality rather than to simply identify with a set of attitudes.

This can be helped by starting with a set of questions for the students to consider.

- What's your name?
- How old are you?
- Are you male or female?
- Are you married or single?
- What's your occupation?
- What do you look like?
- What is your social and educational background?
- What kind of personality do you have?
- What have you been doing today? Where were you, what happened to you – why are you in the casualty department?
- How do you feel about what has happened?

It may be helpful for students to write a personal profile which you can discuss with them individually at a later stage.

5. *Direct students through an improvisation*
- Bring all characters one by one in front of receptionist.
- Create scenes of interaction between waiting patients.
- Bring all characters one by one before the doctor and nurse.

The interaction scenes will have to be carefully orchestrated and controlled by the teacher to avoid having everyone talking at once. Here the 'freeze' technique can be used to good effect, i.e. ask some students to 'freeze' while others go on talking. The teacher's role will be defined by the level of competence of the students. Some students may need a lot of encouragement, prompting, instructions. At this stage do not stop the action to correct grammatical errors as this will destroy the spontaneous flow, but aim for clarity of speech and feed in any language that might be appropriate.

During the first improvisation either record it on tape or make notes of the dialogue.

6. *Shaping and editing:* improvisation involves an element of spontaneity or open-endedness but, moving from drama to theatre now, the action will have to be carefully plotted and a structure imposed. Discuss with the students how to make the play more dramatically effective. What should be left in or developed? What should be left out? Should it be re-arranged in any way?

7. *Scripting:* once the structure has been agreed the play can be properly scripted. This can be done by the group or by the teacher. It will be closely based on the improvisations. Examine the language on the tape or in your notes and suggest ways it can be improved or made more appropriate to the situation.

8. *Staging:* after the first reading of the completed script the play should be staged and the actors' moves and business worked out. This can be achieved by group discussion. Props should also be brought in at this point.

9. *Developing character:* another group discussion would be useful now to consider ways of developing character. For example, how would the drunk walk, sit, speak etc? What tone of voice would the receptionist use?

   Return to the 'personal profiles' which can now be read out and shared. Further improvisations can be set up to deepen the role, for example the quarrel between the receptionist and the boyfriend that created her bad mood. The drunk in the pub before he got drunk. Richard with his wife before he went out to meet his girlfriend, etc. Let the students discuss how they feel about the role they are playing.

10. *Rehearsal:* once the students are completely familiar with their roles and the action of the play they can begin to learn the words and the play can be rehearsed until the performance stage is reached, although you may not wish to take it this far.

    One advantage of the students learning their parts is that it affords an opportunity to concentrate on voice and pronunciation work in a more interesting way than through classroom drilling. Each utterance can be examined from the point of view of articulation, stress, intonation etc. and the appropriateness of the register to the situation and role.

11. *Performance:* if the students do perform their play to an audience keep someone in the 'wings' to prompt when a student drys. You will probably find, however, that because they are thoroughly familiar with the roles and the situation that they will be able to *ad lib* if necessary.

An alternative method of working would be to start with a script and when the students are completely familiar with their roles and the dialogue to move into the creative stage of improvisation, whereby the students use their own language to convey meaning and the mood of the piece.

This approach may be more suitable for a group who are lacking confidence or who find it difficult to express themselves having the script as a prop.

Script 1   Casualty

This script is the result of working through the process I have just described with a group of intermediate ESL students over a period of six weeks. The group met for two hours each week and attendance was good. After doing some warm-up and relaxation exercises at the beginning of the class we would pick up where we had left off the previous week in the development of our play. The group had already been doing drama for two terms and so were quite confident about performing in front of each other and developing character.

The script was based on tape-recordings and teacher's notes. Copies were made of the first draft and one entire lesson was spent on working on the script, polishing and improving and adding natural and idiomatic speech.

The roles were devised by me and I had a general idea of the form I wanted the play to have. I determined the order that the characters were to appear but the resulting interaction and interpretation of the roles was entirely in the hands of the students. For this reason it was a very creative experience for them and an exciting one. They were guided and supported by the teacher as director and the other students as fellow actors and a structure within which to work gradually emerged, but it gave them plenty of scope for self-expression and an opportunity to work on an imaginative level with others.

The roles

1. You are the hospital receptionist. You are very bad-tempered, abrupt and unsympathetic with the patients. You have had a quarrel with your boyfriend and that is why you are in a bad mood. You are tired and bored with your job.
2. You are the nurse. You are very efficient and experienced. You like your job and you are kind and sympathetic with the patients.
3. You are the doctor. You see each patient – ask them questions and suggest treatment. Sometimes you get impatient but you do your job efficiently. You don't like working in 'casualty'. You would like to have your own private practice.

4. You have just been mugged and robbed. You are very agitated and excited. You are concerned about the stolen money. You received a blow on the head which is very painful. You want the police to be called.
5. You are a drunkard who fell in front of a taxi and injured your leg. You are very noisy and rude to everyone, flirting with the women and being generally objectionable. You accuse the doctor of trying to kill you.
6. You are a young policeman. You bring in the drunk man. You are kind but firm.
7. You are a quite well-known actress. You are very aware of your image. You have something in your eye. You think you should be seen first because you think you are very important. You complain about the cold and the uncomfortable surroundings.
8. You are a mother with a child who has swallowed your engagement ring. You are angry with the child and you keep scolding him.
9. You are a child about ten years old. You are very badly behaved and very inquisitive. You keep asking the other patients questions.
10. You are a middle-aged man. You have fallen down a flight of stairs and hurt your back. You are worried about your wife finding out. You don't know how you can explain arriving home so late as you had told her you were visiting your mother but you had taken your secretary out to dinner before you fell down the stairs of her flat.
11. You are someone who has lost your memory. You have wandered into the hospital by chance because you don't know who you are or where to go.
12. You are very depressed because your girlfriend has left you. You tried to kill yourself but your landlady found you and has brought you to the hospital.
13. You are the landlady. You feel sorry for the young man. You are very motherly and try to help him.

Casualty

Scene: The waiting-room in a casualty department of a London hospital. Receptionist sits behind counter, reading a magazine, drinking coffee, yawning.

RECEPTIONIST:	Only midnight.
	[*Man enters staggering, out of breath, holding head.*]
RECEPTIONIST:	What's the matter with you?
MAN:	[*very agitated*] I've, I've, I've been mugged in the street and robbed. I must tell the police.
RECEPTIONIST:	This is a hospital not a police station.

MAN:	I know – but I've lost a lot of money – I must report it.
RECEPTIONIST:	Are you hurt?
MAN:	Yes of course, look at my head – I was hit on the head by these thugs. Look I'm bleeding [*shows her a bloody patch. She draws back.*]
RECEPTIONIST:	What is your name?
MAN:	George Kovaks.
RECEPTIONIST:	How do you spell Kovaks?
KOVAKS:	[*bangs on the counter*] Oh, come on – I'm bleeding to death. Where's the doctor?
RECEPTIONIST:	Doctor is very busy – you'll have to wait your turn. How do you spell Kovaks?
KOVAKS:	Oh my God. K O V A K S.
RECEPTIONIST:	Address?
KOVAKS:	54 Golborne Road, W10. [*He gets out a cigarette and puts it in his mouth*]
RECEPTIONIST:	Please sit over there and wait. [*He goes to light cigarette.*] Sorry, you are not allowed to smoke. [*She points to notice.*]
KOVAKS:	How long have I got to wait?
RECEPTIONIST:	It will be your turn when the patient with the doctor now comes out.
	[*He sits down holds his head – he gets up again and goes back to the receptionist.*]
KOVAKS:	What about calling the police?
RECEPTIONIST:	You'll have to wait until you've seen the doctor.
KOVAKS:	But...
RECEPTIONIST:	Please sit down and wait.
POLICEMAN:	[*helping in a drunk with an injured leg, groaning*] Good evening miss. This man fell in front of a taxi – he's drunk out of his mind.
RECEPTIONIST:	Yes, I can smell it [*drawing back*]. What's his name?
POLICEMAN:	What's your name mate?
DRUNK:	What? Where am I? What's going on? Let me go you swine.
RECEPTIONIST:	Make him sit down over there. Has he any papers on him?
	[*Policeman tries to look in man's pocket – drunk tries to stop policeman – strikes out.*]
DRUNK:	Take your hands off me you bastard.
POLICEMAN:	Watch it mate – you'd better be careful if you don't want to be arrested.
DRUNK:	Are you the police? What's going on – oh my leg is broken – I need a drink.

103

POLICEMAN:	[*to receptionist*]: No papers here – you'll have to wait until he's sober.
	[*Sits man down next to first man – drunk starts moaning and shouting incoherently.*]
KOVAKS:	[*jumps up*]: Excuse me – I've been attacked and robbed. [*To policeman*] I want to report it, officer.
POLICEMAN:	What happened? [*Takes out notebook and makes notes.*]
KOVAKS:	I was walking along the street just now and two blokes came up behind me and bashed me on the head. They pinched all my money.
POLICEMAN:	Where?
KOVAKS:	Just around the corner from here.
POLICEMAN:	Did you get a good look at them?
KOVAKS:	No, not really – it was pretty dark and they came at me from behind.
POLICEMAN:	What did they take?
KOVAKS:	All my money, about thirty quid.
POLICEMAN:	Well I've got the details sir, but there's not much we can do. They must have got clean away by now, but I'll report it at the station anyway. I'll get your name and address from the receptionist.
KOVAKS:	Thanks, officer.
POLICEMAN:	Give me that man's name and address please. [*She passes it to him and he writes it down. He leaves.*]
KOVAKS:	How much longer have I got to wait? I could be dying.
RECEPTIONIST:	It should be soon now. Please sit down. [*Woman enters.*]
WOMAN:	Quick, I've got something in my eye. I'm in terrible agony – I must see a doctor immediately.
RECEPTIONIST:	The doctor is busy – you'll have to wait.
DRUNK:	Hallo darling [*patting seat*] come and sit here next to me. [*She looks and then turns away quickly.*]
WOMAN:	I can't wait – I have to go to a very important party – I must be seen *now*.
RECEPTIONIST:	Impossible.
WOMAN:	Do you know who I am?
RECEPTIONIST:	I don't care if you are the Queen of England. You will still have to wait your turn.
DRUNK:	Who are you darling?
RECEPTIONIST:	What is your name please?
WOMAN:	Loraine Lucille, I'm an actress – surely you recognise me.
RECEPTIONIST:	No, I don't have time to look at actresses.
DRUNK:	Hello Loraine.
LORAINE:	This is dreadful – I can't wait in a place like this.

104

RECEPTIONIST:	Everyone is equal here. What is your address?
LORAINE:	I'm not prepared to reveal it.
RECEPTIONIST:	Very well, please sit down and wait your turn. [*Loraine takes out her cigarettes.*] No smoking.
LORAINE:	I'm not used to this sort of treatment – I shall report you to your superior.
RECEPTIONIST:	As you please.
KOVAKS:	How much longer?
	[*Nurse enters, goes to receptionist's desk, picks up records.*]
NURSE:	George Kovaks. Come this way please. The doctor can see you now.
KOVAKS:	About time too. [*Exit.*]
DRUNK:	Hello nurse – have you got a little drink for me then?
NURSE:	I'll fetch you some black coffee.
DRUNK:	Not coffee. Whiskey.
	[*He gets up and goes to sit next to Loraine.*]
	Hello my lovely. [*Exit Nurse.*]
LORAINE:	Don't touch me you disgusting creature. [*She moves away.*]
DRUNK:	You stuck-up bitch.
RECEPTIONIST:	Please watch your language.
LORAINE:	This place is freezing – haven't you got any heating on?
RECEPTIONIST:	This is not Harley Street – economies have to be made.
LORAINE:	It certainly isn't Harley Street. I usually go to a private doctor but where would I find one at this time of night?
RECEPTIONIST:	Yes, beggers can't be choosers, can they?
DRUNK:	My leg is killing me. [*Looking round.*] Where's that swine that knocked me down? He should pay for this.
RECEPTIONIST:	It was your own fault. The policeman said you fell down in front of the taxi because you were too drunk to stand up.
DRUNK:	That's not true – who's drunk? I'm as sober as a judge.
RECEPTIONIST:	Hmmm.
NURSE:	Here's some black coffee for you. Now behave yourself and stop annoying everybody.
DRUNK:	Thank you nurse. How about a little kiss? [*Nurse leaves.*]
WOMAN WITH CHILD:	[*very agitated*] We need to see a doctor urgently.
RECEPTIONIST:	What's wrong?
WOMAN:	My boy has swallowed my diamond ring.
RECEPTIONIST:	I see. What's his name.
WOMAN:	John.
RECEPTIONIST:	John what?

WOMAN:	John Brown.
RECEPTIONIST:	Where do you live?
	[*Child plays with toy on counter, picks up telephone. Receptionist stops him.*]
WOMAN:	32 Manor Drive, Kilburn. Can we see a doctor now?
RECEPTIONIST:	No you'll have to wait. There are other people before you. Anyway it's not very serious.
WOMAN:	Not serious? That ring is worth £200.
RECEPTIONIST:	How do you know he swallowed it?
WOMAN:	Because I saw him, the little devil. He did it on purpose.
BOY:	No I didn't – I thought it was a sweet.
WOMAN:	Don't tell lies you little swine. [*She smacks him.*]
BOY:	I'm not, I'm not.
RECEPTIONIST:	Stop quarrelling please. Go over there and sit down.
BOY:	[*Goes over to drunk.*] What did you swallow?
MOTHER:	Come away. [*Pulling boy.*]
LORAINE:	Too much alcohol child – that's what he swallowed.
BOY:	What's alcohol?
LORAINE:	Never mind.
BOY:	What's wrong with your eye? It's all red. Why have got all that stuff on your face?
	[*Loraine gets out mirror and looks at herself.*]
WOMAN:	Behave yourself – stop asking questions, you naughty boy. Sit here.
NURSE:	Next patient please.
LORAINE:	That's me.
RECEPTIONIST:	No, it's that gentleman.
LORAINE:	Gentleman, he is not a gentleman – he's just a drunk.
DRUNK:	Who are you calling a drunk? [*Goes to strike her.*]
NURSE:	[*restraining him*] Come with me.
DRUNK:	What are you going to do to me? I don't trust you people in white coats.
NURSE:	Come along.
	[*Doctor's surgery.*]
DOCTOR:	Sit down. Where are his records?
NURSE:	He was too drunk to give his name. He fell in front of a taxi?
DRUNK:	I didn't fall. The taxi tried to kill me.
DOCTOR:	Are you hurt?
DRUNK:	Yes, it's my leg.
DOCTOR:	Let me see.
DRUNK:	Take your hands off me. You're not going to cut off my leg.
DOCTOR:	Don't be so stupid. We only want to have a look. [*He

106

	examines the leg.]
DOCTOR:	It's quite a bad fracture. We shall have to X-ray your leg and probably put it in plaster.
DRUNK:	Plastered? ... I'm not plastered.
DOCTOR:	I said we would have to put your leg in plaster. You can't walk on that leg.
DRUNK:	I don't trust you butchers.
DOCTOR:	Take him to X-ray, nurse, and send in the next patient.
NURSE:	Yes doctor. Come along you.
	[*Receptionist is reading her magazine again. A man approaches.*]
MAN:	Excuse me. I've hurt my back. I must see a doctor.
RECEPTIONIST:	What happened to you?
MAN:	I fell down some stairs.
RECEPTIONIST:	What's your name?
MAN:	Richard Davies.
RECEPTIONIST:	Where do you live?
DAVIES:	48 Freston Road, Wimbledon. I must see a doctor now. I've got to get home before my wife finds out.
RECEPTIONIST:	Finds out what?
DAVIES:	[*confidentially*] Well she thinks I'm visiting my mother but I was really at a girlfriend's flat when I fell down the stairs. If I don't get home soon she'll be suspicious. It's already midnight.
RECEPTIONIST:	Well you'll have to wait like everyone else. We only have one doctor on duty tonight and he's very busy. Please sit down.
DAVIES:	Oh dear, I'm in terrible trouble now.
BOY:	Why are you in trouble – did you tell lies?
MOTHER:	Be quiet.
BOY:	Did the lady push you down the stairs?
MOTHER:	Shut up, Johnnie.
LORAINE:	That child is getting on my nerves. Can't you keep him quiet?
MOTHER:	He's tired. He should be in bed. They should see children first. You shouldn't have to wait with children.
NURSE:	Miss Loraine Lucille please.
LORAINE:	At last. I've been waiting nearly two hours. It's disgusting. I'm frozen stiff.
NURSE:	Doctor will see you now.
	[*Phone rings.*]
RECEPTIONIST [*to Nurse*]:	It's for you.
NURSE:	[*listens*] Yes, I see. [*Puts phone down.*]

	[*To Loraine*] I'm sorry, you'll have to wait a big longer. We are having some trouble with the drunk man. He is fighting the nurses who are trying to put his leg in plaster.
LORAINE:	Oh, really this is too much. [*Stamps her foot.*]
NURSE:	Please be patient. I'll be back soon.
	[*Man enters: wanders towards reception counter.*]
MAN:	I want a single room.
RECEPTIONIST:	What?
MAN:	I want a single room with bath.
RECEPTIONIST:	This isn't a hotel – it's a hospital.
MAN:	Never mind. I need a room.
RECEPTIONIST:	What's wrong with you?
MAN:	I don't know.
RECEPTIONIST:	What's your name?
MAN:	I can't remember.
RECEPTIONIST:	What do you mean, you can't remember?
MAN:	I can't remember my name.
RECEPTIONIST:	Where do you live?
MAN:	I don't know.
RECEPTIONIST:	Have you lost your memory?
MAN:	I can't remember.
RECEPTIONIST:	You're not English are you. Where do you come from?
MAN:	I don't know.
NURSE:	[*to Loraine*] Doctor will see you now.
RECEPTIONIST:	Nurse, this man is suffering from amnesia.
NURSE:	Oh, dear – he'd better see the doctor first then.
LORAINE:	No, certainly not. I'm next.
WOMAN:	[*jumps up*] What about my boy? Children shouldn't have to wait. They are important.
LORAINE:	Nonsense, I'm a famous actress – I'm more important than any of you.
MAN:	[*to Loraine*] I've seen you before.
NURSE:	Where, where have you seen this lady?
MAN:	I don't know. I can't remember.
LORAINE:	He's probably seen me on television. Please let me see the doctor now. My eye is so painful and I must get to my party.
NURSE:	All right. You sit there [*to man*] and try to remember something.
MAN:	What shall I try to remember?
NURSE:	Anything.
BOY:	Did you fall down the stairs too?
MAN:	I can't remember.

DAVIES:	*[to himself]* My wife will kill me when she finds out. What shall I tell her? *[Looks at his watch.]*
BOY:	*[to man, proudly]* I've swallowed a diamond ring. What have you swallowed?
MAN:	I can't remember. I don't think I swallowed anything.
DOCTOR:	Good evening. Please sit down. *[Gets up and helps her to a seat very ingratiatingly.]* I believe you are Loraine Lucille? I'm a great admirer of yours.
LORAINE:	Well, I'm not an admirer of yours or this appalling hospital. I've been kept waiting in a draughty waiting-room for nearly three hours with all sorts of riff-raff.
NURSE:	That's an exaggeration – it was only two hours.
DOCTOR:	I'm so sorry Miss Lucille. If I had known you were waiting I would have seen you immediately. I will reprimand the staff concerned, be assured. Now what seems to be the trouble?
LORAINE:	It's my eye, doctor. I was getting ready to go to a very special party and I was just putting on my false eyelashes when one of the lashes fell into my eye.
DOCTOR:	Oh, you poor dear. Let me see.
LORAINE:	Please be gentle with me doctor.
DOCTOR:	Of course, Miss Lucille. Let me have a closer look. *[Examines eye.]* There you are it's out now.
LORAINE:	But I can still feel it.
DOCTOR:	Only until the soreness wears off. Nurse, take Miss Lucille to bathe her eye and then get her a taxi.
LORAINE:	Thank you doctor. You are the only civilised person I've spoken to in this terrible place. *[Exit.]*
DAVIES:	Can I go next please? I've got to get home before my wife finds out.
RECEPTIONIST:	No you can't. Perhaps this will teach you a lesson not to deceive your wife. Would you like me to phone her and tell her where you are?
DAVIES:	No, no, she mustn't find out.
NURSE:	*[to man]* Have you remembered anything yet?
MAN:	I did remember something, 5 minutes ago, but I've forgotten it now.
WOMAN WITH MAN:	*[Woman enters holding man up. He is staggering.]* This man is very ill. I think he's taken an overdose.
MAN:	Let me die. I don't want to live any more.
RECEPTIONIST:	Attempted suicide?
WOMAN:	Yes, I think so. There was a note. I'm his landlady. I found him on the floor in the bathroom. Wake up. You

	must keep awake.
RECEPTIONIST:	I'll get the nurse immediately. Keep him on his feet.
WOMAN:	[*to Davies*] Help me. [*They walk him up and down.*]
DAVIES:	Come on man, keep walking.
MAN:	Let me die. I want to die. There's no point any more
DAVIES:	Why do you want to die? Oh, my back. [*He keels over.*] I think I am dying too. [*He collapses.*]
MOTHER:	Let me take him. Come on. Life is beautiful, young man, why do you want to die?
BOY:	Is he drunk, mummy? Has he swallowed something?
MAN:	She has left me – I can't live without her. Life means nothing to me now. Let me die.
LANDLADY:	Don't be silly. You'll find another girl. There are plenty more fish in the sea.
MAN:	But I only want her. How can I get her back?
BOY:	[*Gets ring out of his pocket.*] You can give her this ring as a present if you like.
MOTHER:	My God, it's my ring. You bad boy, you didn't swallow it. [*She smacks him.*] [*Boy crys.*]
MAN:	[*jumps up*] I've remembered, I've remembered, I've remembered. [*Comes to centre of stage – everyone moves around him.*]
EVERYONE:	Who are you?
MAN:	Napoleon.

110

Script 2 Hostages

This is an example of a play that could be completed in one or two lessons or it could be developed and scripted by using the same method as was described for *Casualty*.

One essential difference is that in *Casualty* the teacher directed and did not take on an acting role.

In this play the teacher must take on the key role, which is Voice 1, Peter Jones. By adopting a role she may control, guide and shape the play from the inside. The teacher working 'in role' is a useful device that enables her to affect what is happening and extend and challenge the students within the drama process. It will be her task to involve all the students in the action and to get each of them to try to justify, in the context, why he/she should not be chosen as the sacrifice. She must try to move the dialogue along until the situation is resolved.

Method

1. *Allocate the roles* Ask the students to study their role cards and think about their roles but not to discuss them with each other.

2. *Hand out the scripts* Read the introduction aloud but do not look at the dialogue at this point.

3. *Prepare the room* Ask the students to explore the space and take up a position in the room.

When everyone is ready the improvisation can begin. Allow five minutes for the students to talk about and react to the way they have been treated by the terrorists and to tell each other what they have just experienced.

4. *Introduce the telephone call* You answer the telephone. Imagine the voice at the other end is very threatening. He tells you that if the government have not met their demands within two hours one of you will be shot.

He asks you to have a name ready when he phones again of the person who will be sacrificed. He says if no name is chosen you will all be shot.

5. *Work through the scripted part of the action* and then lead the students into the improvisation, which involves telling each other who they are and how they feel about being chosen and what they should do about the situation.

The play should continue unscripted until the situation is resolved. The play ends (you must decide when) with the second phone call demanding your decision.

The improvised scene may be tape-recorded and then scripted by the students if you think it would be a valuable activity as with *Casualty*.

111

The roles

1. Your name is Doctor John Richards. You are 62 years old. You are a widower. You have no children. You are working in cancer research and you think you are on the verge of discovering a new drug to cure cancer victims. You came to this place to attend a medical research conference. You are to speak tomorrow at this conference.

2. Your name is Laura Thomas. You are 23 and you have only been married for one year. You are expecting your first baby. Your husband is a university lecturer. At the time you were taken captive you were resting in your room and your husband had gone out for a walk.

3. Your name is Terry Woods. You have just been released from prison after serving a sentence of five years. You are now 30. You were innocent of the crime you were convicted for but unable to prove your innocence.

4. Your name is Gloria St. John. You are 17. You are a pianist with considerable talent. You have come to this place to take part in an international competition for young musicians. If you do well it will help you in your musical career.

5. Your name is Clare Masters. You are 25. You are blind. You lost your sight in a car accident five years ago in which your husband was killed. You have come to this place to have an operation which might restore your sight. There is a famous surgeon here who thinks he can help you.

6. Your name is Peter Jones. You are married with four young children. Two years ago your wife contracted a rare blood disease and has only a year or two to live. You are a businessman and you are here representing your company to arrange a business contract.

7. Your name is Maisie Graham. You are 50. You are unmarried. You have devoted your life to looking after an invalid mother. She died recently and for the first time in your life you are free to enjoy yourself. You came here to have a holiday and start living your own life again.

8. Your name is Linda Redgrave. You are the daughter of a famous political leader. You are afraid that if the gunmen know your true identity they will choose you as a weapon against the authorities. You are not sure whether to trust the other guests. Should you tell them who you really are?

Hostages

The scene is a hotel lounge on the fifth floor of a small hotel in an unspecified country. The windows, which are double-glazed, are all locked and the one exit, a heavy wooden door, is also locked. In the room

112

are a number of people who are unknown to each other. They are guests at the hotel. They are either sitting or walking about the room looking dazed and shocked.

A few minutes before they had all been forced out of their bedrooms by three armed, masked men and driven into the lounge. The heavy door had then been locked against them. Inside the room there is an internal telephone which is linked to the hotel switchboard.

Gradually, as the occupants recover from their initial shock, they begin to talk about what has just happened, to speculate about what is going to happen and to explore the room.

Suddenly the telephone rings. At first nobody dares pick it up but finally one of the guests lifts the receiver.

VOICE 6:	Hello ... Yes I'm listening ... but ... you can't do that ... oh, I beg you ... for God's sake ... yes, I understand but ... [*The others watch anxiously until the call is finished.*]
VOICE 1:	Well, who was it? What did they say?
VOICE 2:	They're going to kill us aren't they? [*Starts crying.*]
VOICE 4:	Be quiet!
VOICE 6:	It's bad news. I think they're serious – I mean I think they'll do what they say they are going to do and he said that if the government hasn't agreed to release their prisoners in two hours they will shoot one of us ...
VOICE 1:	What prisoners – who are they?
VOICE 3:	This can't be happening – it must be a joke.
VOICE 6:	It's not a joke but the problem now is they've asked us to choose who it should be. One of us will be shot and we have to tell them – they said they would accept whoever we choose.
VOICE 4:	That's generous of them.
VOICE 5:	Surely we can reason with them?
VOICE 6:	No, it's hopeless – he made it quite clear on the phone that they will do it. They're quite capable of murder.
VOICE 3:	They're fanatics.
VOICE 6:	Yes, and ruthless killers. He said if the government doesn't act within the time limit then by killing one hostage they will see that they are serious.
VOICE 1:	Well surely, the government wouldn't let any of us die.
VOICE 3:	Yes, they will get us out.
VOICE 4:	How? – we are on the fifth floor and they have taken over the whole building – there's no way out.
VOICE 7:	Let's smash a window.
VOICE 6:	Don't be stupid – for one thing those windows are unbreakable and for another they would probably come

	in and shoot the lot of us.
VOICE 4:	Well, what are we going to do?
VOICE 6:	Well, we'd better start thinking. They are going to ring back in half an hour and they want a name and description of the person we have chosen to give to the government.
VOICE 1:	How can we choose – we don't even know each other's names.
VOICE 6:	Well, let's try to be calm. We must tell each other who we are and decide whose name to give. We must give a name otherwise he said they will probably kill all of us.
VOICE 3:	What ... you've just invented that – you never said that before.
VOICE 6:	It's true. I didn't want to frighten you before but we must talk now.

Comment:

I have done this play, which is about facing issues and solving a problem, with three different groups and although it was presented to them open-ended in all cases the conclusion they reached was the same. The students, after much discussion, decided not to negotiate with the terrorists. They refused to choose anyone from their group, saying that this would put them on the same level as their murderers. Whether they would adopt such a high moral tone in real life is debatable but it did show group solidarity, which is something that invariably develops within a drama class. One may argue that the situation of hostages is outside students' everyday experience and therefore is not relevant, but terrorism exists in the world we live in and is therefore an interesting subject to consider. It is also a useful dramatic vehicle with which to get an emotional response to a situation. In problem-solving drama the students can discover why people behave as they do and they can be encouraged to reflect on their own behaviour. A fictitious situation outside their normal experience will also facilitate language development, since they will of necessity be searching for language appropriate to the situation.

Discussion about the drama should follow as an integral part of the lesson for, without pause for reflection, the work could be rather superficial.

Script 3   Strike? (for ESL students)

This play arose out of a discussion on trade unions with a class taking a course in 'British Life and Institutions'. Some of the students in this class were also in my drama class and, after some discussion on trade unionism in Britain, it seemed an almost natural progression to make up a play and act out a situation involving workers in dispute with their employer and to show what role the union had to play in resolving the matter. This is drama in education where the drama is intended to educate and inform through physical, emotional and intellectual identification with the subject. To experience imaginatively what it feels like to be cold, miserable, underpaid and exploited surely adds another dimension to our understanding of human behaviour and brings the subject to life.

The first time I explored this theme with ESL students I did not assign any particular roles, but simply suggested that we were all workers in a small factory. One person was chosen to play the part of the villain of the piece, Mr Smith, and he sat aside and listened. I asked them to spend five minutes creating for themselves the atmosphere and the environment. I asked them to imagine they were very cold; they were trying to use machines that were old and hard to handle; the light in the room was poor; the space they had to work in was cramped.

When they had established a sense of the place for themselves I asked them to start chatting about their situation while they worked. In this case I was teacher 'in role', one of them, an ordinary worker, but leading the conversation towards a discussion of their appalling conditions and what they were going to do about it. Once the students' interest has been caught and their imaginations engaged the teacher can gradually withdraw, that is, take a less active part and simply prod and push when necessary to keep the drama moving.

In this instance the students became quite animated and determined to approach the boss and state their case, which they did most adequately. New words were sought – 'negotiate', 'redundant', 'better working conditions', etc. The introduction of much language in drama arises out of a genuine need on the part of the student to use that word or utterance for the first time, and I am convinced that is a much more valid and creative way of acquiring language through necessity than being fed it with a spoon.

Drama also reveals what the students already know and where they are in their language development and is therefore a very useful diagnostic tool for the teacher.

A tape-recording of the improvisation was made, but in this case we did not write down a script.

Script 3   Strike? (for native speakers)

This play is based on the same theme, but this time a structure is imposed and the students are given clearly defined roles and an opportunity to work on character. Everything they say and the attitude they adopt within the play will be determined by the role they are playing. Frances will be outspoken and determined to take action whilst Maria, because of her status and vulnerability, might want to accept the *status quo* (see roles). Differences of opinion might lead to some dramatic tension within the group which is exactly what one hopes will happen. If you are working with an experienced group you might like to let them work on this play by themselves and then show you their finished product, or you might like to sit in and offer advice and suggestions when needed. If the group is not very confident then it is probably best to take a role and guide the drama from the inside.

Although the play has been given a structure do not insist that the students adhere to it strictly if something more interesting seems to be developing. Students are quite capable of creating their own plays.

This is an improvisation for six people.

The scene is a small workshop in a basement somewhere in London where several women of various ages are making children's garments on old-fashioned, outdated sewing machines. The space is very cramped, the room is extremely cold and badly lit and is generally very dirty and depressing.

The roles

Jane   a middle-aged woman with three children. She is the breadwinner as her husband has a serious heart condition and is on permanent sick-leave with a very small pension. She works long hours to support her family.

Sarah   a young mother with a husband who has a drinking problem and he doesn't support her very well. She is pregnant for the second time and is worried about money.

Frances   a younger woman, unmarried, quite political and keen on women's rights. Through her efforts the boss has recently, but very reluctantly, allowed the women to join a union. She is their shop steward.

Maria   a Spanish migrant worker who feels very vulnerable. She must keep this job or she could lose her work permit, but she is quite slow and not very experienced. She has to send money home to her family in Spain.

Nina   a West Indian. She lives with her parents who emigrated to Britain twenty years ago. She was five when she came to England. She is good and efficient at her work but because there is so much unemployment she doesn't think she would find another job very easily.

116

Mr Smith   the boss. He owns this small business. He is middle-aged. He is dominated by his wife who takes most of his profits to buy expensive clothes etc. He is mean to his staff.

> Method:
> Discuss the factory and the various roles with the students and let them choose whom they would like to play.
>   The purpose of the improvisation will be to resolve the problem of their bad working conditions, particularly the cold, and also to do something about their wages, which are very low. They are not paid a proper wage. They get 50p per garment and under these conditions a garment could take at least one hour to make, therefore their output is very poor.

Scene 1   The women discuss their situation at work and they also talk about their personal problems.
    They decide to confront the boss.
Scene 2   In Mr Smith's office. Frances has an interview. She is representing the other women.
    Does she manage to persuade him to make changes or not?
Scene 3   She reports back to the women. Are they satisfied? If not what do they decide to do next?

Strike?

Scene 1   In the workshop

JANE: God, it's freezing in here. I'll have to put my coat on again in a minute. I feel chilled to the bloody bone. It's probably warmer outside.

NINA: I've got three sweaters on and two pairs of tights and I'm still cold.

SARAH: My hands are frozen – look at them Jane – they've gone all blue.

JANE: So they have. Here, let me rub them for you.
[*She rubs Sarah's hands between her own.*]
You should be warm in your condition. Poor kid could die of frostbite before it's even seen daylight. When's the baby due anyway?

SARAH: In three months. God help the poor little devil. It won't have much to look forward to.

NINA: Hey, perhaps it'll be a blue baby – do you get it? Blue hands, blue baby. [*She laughs.*]

117

SARAH:	I don't think that's very funny, Nina.
NINA:	Sorry, I was only joking. No need to be so touchy.
JANE:	Well, you shouldn't make jokes like that. It's in very poor taste.
NINA:	Alright. I said I'm sorry. Let's change the subject.
FRANCES:	We shouldn't have to work in these conditions – it's like the sweat shops of the 30s.
JANE:	What do you know about the 30s at your age?
FRANCES:	I know. I saw a programme about those days on TV. The places they showed were just like it is here. Anyway my dad's told me plenty of things about the depression and it's all happening again, you'll see. History repeats itself.
MARIA:	Oh dear. I can't work very fast. I'm too cold. Mr Smith will be angry with me again. He said he'd sack me if I didn't work better.
NINA:	Sod him. I'd like to see him working in these conditions.
JANE:	Why don't you go back to Spain, Maria? It can't be any worse there than it is here and at least you'd have your family. You must be lonely on your own here.
MARIA:	Oh no. There's no work at all where I come from and I must stay and help my family. I've got five brothers and sisters and no dad.
SARAH:	Where's your dad, love?
MARIA:	He dead two years ago.
SARAH:	You mean he *died* two years ago?
MARIA:	Yes he dead.
JANE:	Look – all I've produced this morning is five dresses – that's 50p per dress. £2.50 for three hours work – it's a waste of time. How am I going to pay my bills? – There's gas and electricity this month.
FRANCES:	It's about time we got a proper wage like everybody else – not payment by results. It's a system that went out years ago before people knew what their rights were. I bet he wouldn't treat us like this if we were men.
JANE:	No, he thinks he can push us around because we're only women. Sheer exploitation, that's what it is.
NINA:	Well, if we don't get some more heat in here we might as well pack up. I shall never get used to the cold in this country. In Jamaica it's lovely and hot.
FRANCES:	What do you know about it? You were only a little kid when you left there.
NINA:	I can still remember.
JANE:	What's the temperature in here?
SARAH:	Only 10 degrees and its only the beginning of the winter.

118

	Think what it will be like in January.
NINA:	Well you won't be here then, will you Sarah?
SARAH:	Why not?
NINA:	Because of your baby. You'll have to give up work then, won't you?
SARAH:	I can't. I shall have to go on working after and let my mum look after the baby – she doesn't mind – she already looks after my other kid.
NINA:	Well, I'd rather give up work and look after my own kids if I got married.
SARAH:	What chance have I got with a husband who spends all his time in the pub? He drinks most of what he earns. We need this money, little as it is.
JANE:	I bet old Smith won't keep the job for you.
FRANCES:	Yes, he must. It's the law now I think – that a woman can have maternity leave and later get her old job back. It's three months or maybe six.
NINA:	Well, I can't imagine anyone in their right mind wanting to come back to this dump.
MARIA:	Well, it's not easy to find any job now, especially for women.
JANE:	You know, going back to the cold, I would have thought it was against the law for us to work in such low temperatures.
SARAH:	I think we should complain to old Smith. I bet he's nice and cosy in his warm comfortable office. One miserable little gas fire that's all we've got and the light is so bad I can hardly see what I'm doing.
NINA:	He's a mean bastard. All he thinks about is how much money we can make for him.
FRANCES:	Well, we'd make much more if this place was properly heated. Can't we do something?
NINA:	Yes, set fire to it. That would warm it up a bit. [*She laughs.*]
JANE:	Be serious. Surely we can do something. Don't forget we're in the union now and you're our shop steward. You go and talk to him. Tell him we want better working conditions and we want proper money.
FRANCES:	How much money?
MARIA:	Well, we'd have to, what do you call it?
JANE:	Negotiate.
MARIA:	Yes, that's it, 'negoatiate' for a better wage.
NINA:	It's 'negotiate' Maria, not 'negoatiate.'
MARIA:	Yes that's what I said 'negoatiate'.

FRANCES:	Shall I go up then?
ALL:	Yes, go on.
JANE:	Tell him our demands.
NINA:	Don't be soft with him now.
FRANCES:	Do you think you can do it better?
NINA:	No, no, you're the shop steward. It's up to you. Anyway you can put things better than the rest of us.

Scene 2

FRANCES:	Mr Smith, can I see you?
SMITH:	Yes my dear, come in. How are you?
FRANCES:	I'm not feeling very well. I've got a cold.
SMITH:	Well there are a lot of colds about at the moment. My wife has one. You'd better keep yourself warm.
FRANCES:	Well that's the problem – how can we keep ourselves warm in that workshop? It's freezing.
SMITH:	Is it? I can't understand that. You've got a nice little gas fire. I bought it new, well nearly new, just last month. It cost £10.
FRANCES:	It's not at all adequate – it only heats one corner and the rest of the room is freezing. Sarah's hands are blue.
SMITH:	Yes, well I believe that young lady has poor circulation. She should do more exercise. Anyway she'll have to leave soon.
FRANCES:	We are *all* cold, not just Sarah – feel my hands.
SMITH:	Yes, yes a bit cold. So what do you want me to do?
FRANCES:	Put in a proper central heating system.
SMITH:	You must be joking. That would cost a fortune. Do you think I'm made of money? The amount you girls are producing hardly pays the bills. I'm almost going out of business. Too much gossiping and complaining instead of doing your work, it seems to me.
FRANCES:	But don't you see we could produce much more if the conditions were better? We are too cold to work fast.
SMITH:	Sorry my dear, nothing I can do I'm afraid. Perhaps one of you could bring a heater in from home if you're cold. I mean one of those oil stoves. You'd have to pay for the fuel yourselves of course.
FRANCES:	That's no solution.
SMITH:	Anything else? I haven't much time.
FRANCES:	Yes, we want to have a proper wage and not payment by results. The system here is like something out of the dark ages. Nobody does piecework nowadays.

120

SMITH:	Nonsense. Anyway, you'd all get less if I paid you a flat wage, believe me. That Maria produces hardly anything. Do you think she should get the same as the others?
FRANCES:	Yes, we all want a fair wage and, anyway, there is a legal minimum that you would have to pay.
SMITH:	I suppose it's that Union putting all these revolutionary ideas in your heads. I knew it would only bring trouble. Well, my dear, if you want a fixed wage one of you would have to go and you'd have to double production. I can't afford to pay you all just to sit around gossiping.
FRANCES:	That's not fair. We all work as hard as we can in these conditions.
SMITH:	Well, I haven't got time to argue with you now. I've got a meeting in ten minutes so I think you'd better get back to work. Thank you for coming to see me – I always like to keep in touch with my staff.
FRANCES:	Well, I'm not very happy. I'll tell the others what you said but they won't like it.
SMITH:	Yes, yes, well none of us is very happy in this present economic climate. We're in a recession don't forget. Lucky to have jobs at all.

Scene 3   In the workshop

EVERYONE:	Well, what did he say?
JANE:	You don't look very pleased.
FRANCES:	He said no more heating – he can't afford it?
SARAH:	Mean bastard. So he's not going to do anything for us?
FRANCES:	No, he said we could bring in our own heaters if we liked and pay for the extra heating.
NINA:	What a cheek!
JANE:	What about wages?
FRANCES:	He said it would be less than we get now.
MARIA:	It couldn't be. What about minimum wages?
NINA:	Exactly.
FRANCES:	He said he'd have to get rid of one of us if we insisted on wages.
MARIA:	That would be me I expect.
FRANCES:	Probably, he said you're the slowest.
JANE:	Never mind, she's still learning. No one's going to get the sack – we must stick together. Don't let that swine bully us.
NINA:	Let's go on strike.
SARAH:	Don't be daft. We'd get no money at all then and he'd

probably sack us anyway.

MARIA: Oh dear, would he? I can't afford to be out of work.

NINA: Doesn't the Union pay you strike pay if you go on strike?

FRANCES: Yes, if they have sufficient funds but only if the strike is official.

JANE: What do you mean, love?

FRANCES: Well we must get our Union to approve the strike first. If we just say we're on strike its unofficial and we may not get any Union support. But I think we have a good case, so we should see our branch secretary and let him negotiate with Smith on our behalf and if we have a good case the Union will fight for us.

NINA: Well, what are we waiting for? You ring him and get him to come over.

JANE: Yes, let's call him. Women unite. We have nothing to lose but frozen fingers.

[*Three weeks later.*]

UNION OFFICIAL: I was impressed with this case. These women were being exploited. Their working conditions were dreadful and their pay was much too low. I negotiated with Smith. He was very unco-operative at first but gradually I made him see that the working conditions and the method of payment contravened present industrial laws. Reluctantly he made some improvements in the workshop – better heating and lighting and he introduced a proper wage structure. Wages were not high but the women at least achieved better working conditions and more financial security and no one was sacked.

122

Script 4   Shoplifter

This play was written for an ESL class by another student attending a creative writing class.

Before working on the play I tried to prepare the students in various ways. First, we did some role-play on 'accusation' and 'denial' in which the accused had to defend themselves and convince their accuser that they were innocent. We discussed what it felt like to be wrongly accused. 'It was very upsetting.' 'It made me angry and frustrated.' 'I was indignant', etc. We then discussed the theme of shoplifting and considered what sort of people did this thing. Were they poor people who stole out of necessity? Were they criminals? Were they seeking attention? Were they psychologically confused? We did a further series of role-play where the shoplifter was being interviewed by a psychiatrist who was trying to discover her motivation, for example, fulfilling the need for excitement, compensating for neglect by her husband, habit acquired through upbringing, etc.

We paid a visit to a local magistrates' court to soak up the atmosphere and to get acquainted with the procedures. When we finally came to the play the students had gained many insights and had considered the subject thoroughly. We read the play a couple of times, recorded it and listened to our own recording.

Shoplifter

Cast:
Vera Redgrave – Store Detective
Sandra Phillips – (Culprit) Young Girl
Margaret Williams – Manageress

Scene 1
Outside Bradleys, a very exclusive ladies' wear shop in the Marylebone High Street, W1

V. REDGRAVE:	Do you mind if I look inside your basket?
SANDRA:	Eh!
V. REDGRAVE:	Can I look inside your basket?
SANDRA:	Why do you want to look inside my basket?
V. REDGRAVE:	We have reason to believe that there's a pair of french knickers in it which have not been paid for.
SANDRA:	What french knickers? You don't know what you're talking about.
V. REDGRAVE:	Could you please step into the Manageress's office?
SANDRA:	No I won't. I've done nothing wrong.
V. REDGRAVE:	This way please [*holding Sandra's arm*].

Inside Manageress's Office

M. WILLIAMS: Can I have your basket please?

SANDRA: I haven't done anything wrong.

V. REDGRAVE: Give Mrs Williams the basket.

SANDRA: All right.

M. WILLIAMS: Miss Redgrave, would you please check the contents of the basket?

V. REDGRAVE: Here they are, here are the french knickers.

SANDRA: How did they get into my basket? You must have put them in there.

M. WILLIAMS: Don't be a silly girl. We just found them in your basket.

V. REDGRAVE: I saw you pick them up earlier and watched to see whether you would either put them back or pay for them. You did neither.

SANDRA: What are you going to do with me?

M. WILLIAMS: Miss Redgrave, will you please call the police?

V. REDGRAVE: Yes, right away Mrs Williams.
[*Sandra bursts into tears as Miss Redgrave telephones.*]

V. REDGRAVE: They'll be here shortly.

Scene 2

Sandra Phillips, having been arrested for shoplifting from Bradley's (a smart ladies' wear shop in Marylebone High Street) is now at Marylebone Police Station. She is accused of taking a pair of silk french knickers.

Enter Detective Inspector Frost, Detective Inspector Savage, WPC Collins and Sandra.

FROST: OK Sandra, sit yourself down – and for God's sake STOP crying.

SANDRA: [*sitting at a table*] Whatever I say you won't believe me. You believe what that woman said, don't you?

SAVAGE: Now Sandra, try to calm down. We're not here to judge you, you know, that's for the magistrate ...

SANDRA: How long must I stay here?

WPC: Sandra we have to take quite a few details from you before we can make any progress at all. [*She hands Frost a piece of paper, which he inserts into his typewriter.*]

FROST: OK Sandra, you're full name?

SANDRA: Sandra Philips.

FROST: No middle name?

SANDRA: No.

FROST: Date of birth?

SANDRA:	October 24th 1957.
FROST:	And where were you born?
SANDRA:	I dunno, some hospital somewhere ...
FROST:	I must admit I had a suspicion that you MIGHT have been born in a HOSPITAL, but WHERE Sandra, WHERE?
SANDRA:	I don't know – some hospital in London.
FROST:	Sandra, I didn't ask WHICH hospital you were born in. I don't CARE which hospital – I only asked WHERE, and the answer is London. It might save time if you could remember that, should you ever be asked again.
SANDRA:	It might have been that one in Praed Street ...
FROST:	Give me strength! Right. Address?
SANDRA:	D'you mean MY address?
FROST:	Yes, oddly enough.
SANDRA:	15 Priory Park Road.
FROST:	Where's that?
SANDRA:	Kilburn.
FROST:	Postal code?
SANDRA:	It's N.W.6 I think.
FROST:	N.W.6.
SANDRA:	I've got to pick my baby up soon you know.
SAVAGE:	You didn't say you had a child.
SANDRA:	You never asked. Anyway I have, and I'm s'posed to pick him up 'bout 5 o'clock.
SAVAGE:	Where is he?
SANDRA:	At my Mum's. She gets terribly worried if I'm late.
SAVAGE:	Is she on the telephone?
SANDRA:	No. Well she is, but it's been cut off ...
SAVAGE:	All right, what's her address?
SANDRA:	Why d'you want to know?
SAVAGE:	So that we can send an officer round to let her know you're all right.
SANDRA:	Oh no, oh please don't do that. Oh please, please don't do that.
SAVAGE:	Now don't be a silly girl. Your mother would have to know anyway. Be a good girl and give me the address. Nothing will be said to upset your mother, I promise.
SANDRA:	What d'you mean? Just opening the front door and seeing one of you lot standing there's going to upset her, isn't it?
SAVAGE:	Is it? Why's that, Sandra?
SANDRA:	Well you're not exactly likely to be bringing good news are you?
FROST:	[to Savage] Ask a silly question!

SAVAGE:	Look Sandra, just give us the address, will you?
SANDRA:	Oh, all right. It's 31 Kingsgate Place.
SAVAGE:	Which is where?
SANDRA:	Just off Kilburn High Road.
FROST:	[to Savage] I'll phone through to Kilburn nick and get them to send a man round, John. [Frost exits]
SAVAGE:	How old is your son?
SANDRA:	Terry? He's three, just three.
SAVAGE:	Where's his father?
SANDRA:	I don't know! OR care. Lousy sod. Left us when Terry was three months.
SAVAGE:	How've you managed?
SANDRA:	Social Security. And I do a bit of part time work sometimes ...
FROST:	[re-entering] OK. That's all taken care of. Now where'd we got to? I was s'posed to be off an hour ago. Wonderful isn't it? Now Sandra, any previous?
SANDRA:	Any what?
FROST:	Any previous convictions?
SANDRA:	No.
FROST:	No? OK, we'll see. Do a CRO on her, will you, John? Oh and John, see if you can rustle up a cup of something will you?
SAVAGE:	Sandra, what d'you fancy, tea or coffee?
SANDRA:	I'll have a tea please.
FROST:	Tea it is! Thanks John.
	[John Savage exits]
FROST:	[to WPC Collins] Right, I'll go and organise the mug shots! Lock the door and search her. [Exits.]
	[WPC Collins locks the door.]
WPC:	Right Sandra, could you take everything off please?
SANDRA:	What for?
WPC:	It's just routine. For all I know you might have a second pair of french knickers secreted on your person.
SANDRA:	Well I haven't.
WPC:	Good. Then you've got nothing to worry about have you? Now, undress please.
SANDRA:	[undressing] D'you do this to everybody you arrest?
WPC:	It depends ...
SANDRA:	What on?
WPC:	Everything off please Sandra ...
SANDRA:	Honestly, what a liberty. There! Happy now?
WPC:	OK, get dressed Sandra.
SANDRA:	See, I told you.

WPC:	Just get dressed.
	[WPC goes and unlocks door. After a moment Savage enters with Frost.]
FROST:	*[to Savage]* So no previous?
SAVAGE:	Not according to CRO.
FROST:	Right. *[to WPC Collins]* All clean was she?
WPC:	Yes, Sir.
FROST:	Good. OK Sandra, you've got to have your dabs taken now, off you go with Mr Savage.
SANDRA:	My what?
SAVAGE:	Finger prints, Sandra, finger prints. And we'll have to take photographs of you.
SANDRA:	Oh my God, I'm never going to get out of here am I?
SAVAGE:	Come along, there's a good girl. You can have your tea when we get back.
SANDRA:	You think I'll have earned it by then, do you?
FROST:	Now don't start getting clever young lady, or you may regret it.
	[Sandra and Savage exit left, and Frost and WPC exit right.]
	[Marylebone Police Station, ten minutes later: Frost and Savage are seated at a table, with Sandra facing them, also seated.]
FROST:	Now then Sandra, let's go back over today. You say you left the kid with your Mum and you took a tube to Baker Street, right?
SANDRA:	Yes.
FROST:	You walked down Baker Stret, and eventually you ended up in Marylebone High Street, right?
SANDRA:	Yes. I just decided I was gonna have a day to myself. A day without Terry ... I thought it would make a nice change ... It's made a change all right, but I don't know if 'nice' is the right word ...
SAVAGE:	Sandra, tomorrow you will go before Marylebone Magistrates Court and you will be charged with shoplifting ...
SANDRA:	But ...
SAVAGE:	Sandra listen! Nothing you can say or do now will prevent that. And how you plead tomorrow is a matter for you ...
FROST:	And your conscience.
SANDRA:	I didn't take those bloody knickers, but I told you that the minute I saw you. I've told you it till I'm blue in the face. You don't believe me, do you? So what's the point?

127

FROST:	Sandra, speaking personally I don't care how you plead, or what you do – I'm just doing my job here. But if you DID it for Christ's sake plead 'Guilty' and get it over with because it'll be much worse for you if you plead 'Not Guilty' and the court thinks you are ...
SANDRA:	Why?
SAVAGE:	Well the whole thing'll get dragged out and if you're still found guilty then you'll get a heavier fine.
SANDRA:	I haven't any money anyway. Can't get blood out of a stone can you?
FROST:	If you plead 'Not Guilty' it won't be dealt with tomorrow.
SANDRA:	Why not?
FROST:	Because you'll have to get a solicitor to defend you.
SANDRA:	A solicitor! Of course! I never thought of that. Yes! Of course I must have a solicitor.
FROST:	Oh well, that's about as far as we can go this evening. I believe your mother is on her way to collect you.
SANDRA:	My Mum, coming here?
SAVAGE:	Well you don't want to spend the night in a cell do you Sandra? She's going to stand bail for you, and bring you to court in the morning.

Scene 3

Sandra Philips, having been accused of shoplifting, appears at Marylebone Magistrates Court: she stands in the dock.

Cast:
Sandra Philips
D.I. Frost
Vera Redgrave (store detective for Bradley's)
Miss Howell (solicitor defending Sandra Philips)
Magistrate
Clerk of the Court

CLERK:	Sandra Philips, you are charged that you did, on the 5th of November last, steal a pair of french knickers from Bradley's in Marylebone High Street. How do you plead, Guilty or Not Guilty?
SANDRA:	Not Guilty.
CLERK:	Very well. Does she have a solicitor acting for her?
MISS HOWELL:	[standing up] Yes sir, I am acting for the defendant.
CLERK:	Very well. If the police officer in question would take the stand?

MISS HOWELL:	I believe we are starting with the store detective sir.
CLERK:	Very well, if she could take the stand.
	[*Enter Vera Redgrave. She goes into the witness box.*]
CLERK:	What religion are you?
V. REDGRAVE:	Church of England.
CLERK:	Take the Bible in your right hand and read the words printed on the card.
V. REDGRAVE:	I swear by Almighty God that the evidence I shall give to this court will be the truth, the whole truth, and nothing but the truth.
CLERK:	Is your name Vera Redgrave?
V. REDGRAVE:	It is.
CLERK:	And what is your occupation?
V. REDGRAVE:	I work as a store detective for Bradleys.
CLERK:	Now Miss Redgrave, could you tell the court, in your own words, what happened on November the 5th?
V. REDGRAVE:	Well sir, it was about 3.30 in the afternoon, I had just had a coffee, when this girl came into the shop.
CLERK:	Do you see that girl in this courtroom?
V. REDGRAVE:	Yes sir, the same girl that's standing there. [*Points to Sandra.*]
CLERK:	Yes, go on.
V. REDGRAVE:	She was carrying a shopping basket, and a handbag, Anyway, she started looking round and then she picked out about five items ...
MAGISTRATE:	What were these items?
V. REDGRAVE:	French knickers sir – Then she asked if she could try them on.
CLERK:	Yes.
V. REDGRAVE:	Mrs Williams said she could.
MAGISTRATE:	Mrs Williams being?
V. REDGRAVE:	She's the manageress. Anyway Mrs Williams told her she could, so she went into a changing room ... After about five minutes she came out and said they weren't right, and she'd leave it. But I noticed she only gave four pairs back to Mrs Williams.
CLERK:	So what did you then do?
V. REDGRAVE:	I waited till she'd walked out of the shop, then I followed her out and asked if I could look in her basket.
CLERK:	Yes ...
V. REDGRAVE:	The fifth pair of knickers was in her basket.
CLERK:	Yes, go on.
V. REDGRAVE:	So I took her back into the shop, and Mrs Williams called the police.

129

CLERK:	I see. Does the defence wish to cross-examine?
MISS HOWELL:	Yes. Miss Redgrave, can you tell us, how did Miss Philips react when you found the knickers in her basket?
V. REDGRAVE:	Well she PRETENDED to be surprised, like they all do!
MISS HOWELL:	How do you know my client was 'pretending'?
V. REDGRAVE:	Well – as I say, that's what they all do.
MISS HOWELL:	Miss Redgrave, I put it to you that she may genuinely have been surprised. I mean, if it HAD been an accident and the knickers HAD fallen into her basket (as I hope to prove to be the case), surprise would have been a perfectly natural reaction, would it not?
V. REDGRAVE:	Maybe – but I'm sure she was pretending.
MISS HOWELL:	Miss Redgrave, you are not here to give us your opinions, only the facts, if you please. Now, did my client offer any resistance when you asked her to go back into the shop with you?
V. REDGRAVE:	No, not really.
MISS HOWELL:	What do you mean, 'not really'?
V. REDGRAVE:	I mean, well no, she didn't.
MISS HOWELL:	She came quite willingly?
V. REDGRAVE:	Yes.
MISS HOWELL:	And what did she say?
V. REDGRAVE:	She kept saying it was a mistake – but they all say that.
MAGISTRATE:	Miss Redgrave would you be good enough to confine yourself to the matter in question?
V. REDGRAVE:	Yes sir, I'm sorry.
MISS HOWELL:	So my client insisted that it was a mistake?
V. REDGRAVE:	Yes.
MISS HOWELL:	And then what happened?
V. REDGRAVE:	Then the police arrived. They asked us what had happened, and we told them, and then they took her away.
MISS HOWELL:	Thank you Miss Redgrave. No further questions.
CLERK:	You may step down.
	[*Exit Vera Redgrave. D.I. Frost now takes the stand.*]
CLERK:	What religion are you?
FROST:	C. of E.
CLERK:	Take the Bible in your right hand and read the words on the card.
FROST:	I swear by Almighty God that the evidence I shall give to this court shall be the truth, the whole truth, and nothing but the truth.
CLERK:	Name and occupation.
FROST:	Brian Frost. Detective Inspector attached to

	Marylebone Police Station.
CLERK:	Will you tell us about the afternoon of the 5th of November?
FROST:	Yes sir. [*Consults his notebook.*]
	At 3.45 we got a call to go to Bradley's in Marylebone High Street. We arrived shortly after 4 o'clock and were informed that the defendant had left the shop with a pair of french knickers which she had not paid for. I therefore arrested the defendant, and cautioned her. We then took her down to the station for questioning, and we allowed her to go at 7.25 pm when her mother arrived to stand surety for her.
CLERK:	Thank you officer. Does the defence wish to cross-examine?
MISS HOWELL:	Yes sir. Officer, did Miss Philips say anything after you cautioned her?
FROST:	She kept repeating that she hadn't taken the item. She was very upset.
MISS HOWELL:	And you then took her down to the station for questioning?
FROST:	We did.
MISS HOWELL:	Officer, you would agree, would you not, that Miss Philips is a young woman of good character?
FROST:	Yes.
MISS HOWELL:	And it would be fair to say, would it not, that she was completely co-operative with you, and answered all your questions?
FROST:	Oh yes. I got on extremely well with her.
MISS HOWELL:	Thank you officer, no further questions.
CLERK:	You may stand down. Is the defendant taking the stand?
MISS HOWELL:	Yes Sir.
	[*Sandra Philips goes into the witness box.*]
CLERK:	Is your name Sandra Philips, and do you live at 15 Priory Park Road, N.W.6?
SANDRA:	Yes.
MISS HOWELL:	Sandra, will you tell us exactly what happened after you entered Bradley's shop?
SANDRA:	Well, I was having a bit of a day out. My Mum was looking after my little boy, so I thought I'd go shopping. Anyway I came to this shop ...
MAGISTRATE:	Do you mean the shop Bradley's?
SANDRA:	Yes sir. So I came to Bradleys, and I thought maybe I could just afford to get myself a pair of french knickers – so I went in ...

131

MISS HOWELL:	Yes, go on Sandra.
SANDRA:	I picked out a few, and went into the changing-room and started trying them on. then I looked at the labels, and I suddenly realised that they were more than I could afford, so I carried them back out – as I thought *all* of them, and I left the shop. The next thing I know this woman comes out of the shop after me and takes this pair of knickers out of my basket.
MISS HOWELL:	Did you put those knickers into your basket?
SANDRA:	No! I swear I didn't on my little boy's life. They must have fallen in there accidentally without me noticing.
MISS HOWELL:	Was there any thing else in your basket?
SANDRA:	There was a *Daily Mirror* and a pair of gloves.
MISS HOWELL:	Might it be that the knickers had fallen underneath the newspaper, which is why you did not notice them?
SANDRA:	I don't know. They may've done. I didn't look. The first I knew about them was when the store detective came and fished them out.
MISS HOWELL:	How did you feel then?
SANDRA:	I felt AWFUL. I could see she didn't believe me. She wouldn't even listen to me – she just marched me back into the shop and the other one called the p'lice.
MISS HOWELL:	Do you agree that, while you were in the changing room, it would have been quite easy for you to have put the knickers into your basket without being seen?
SANDRA:	Oh yes I do. But if I HAD been going to steal them I wouldn't have done it that way.
MISS HOWELL:	Oh, how would you have done it?
SANDRA:	I'd have put them on!
MISS HOWELL:	And what you did in fact was to TRY them on, then take them off with the intention of returning them?
SANDRA:	Yes. And I'll tell you another thing. If I HAD taken them I wouldn't have been lingering about outside the shop for that woman to come and grab hold of me. She wouldn't have seen me for dust!
MISS HOWELL:	Thank you Sandra, no further questions.
	[*Sandra returns to the dock.*]
MISS HOWELL:	Sir, I shall be very brief. My client, a young lady of good character, denies the charge of stealing the knickers in question. She readily admits that it would have been possible for her to have done so in the manner suggested, but, sir, I think she makes a valid point in remarking that it would have been much simpler for her to have kept the knickers on, and make a run for it after leaving the shop.

132

It is my submission, sir, that unfortunately for my client, the knickers slipped into her basket without her having the slightest knowledge of it. The prosecution have, I submit, fallen very short of proving beyond any reasonable doubt, that my client INTENTIONALLY stole the knickers.

CLERK: [*to Sandra Philips*] Stand please.

MAGISTRATE: I must confess that I am not particularly impressed by the fact that you repeatedly protested your innocence, both in the shop Bradley's and at the police station. After all, you had nothing to lose by so doing. On the other hand I AM impressed by the way you say you would have carried out the theft, had that indeed been your intention. I do not believe it was. Case dismissed.

10
Directing a play

This is an activity for an advanced group who have had quite a lot of ESL drama experience.

Method:

Choose a theme, for example: the seven deadly sins

PRIDE ANGER ENVY LUST AVARICE SLOTH GLUTTONY

Discuss the seven deadly sins and define their meaning.

Choose seven students to be directors.

Each director is given one of the above sins and is asked to devise a situation which will dramatically illustrate the meaning. From the group they can choose actors to be in their play. The play should last about ten minutes. In groups they discuss their ideas.

For example, ENVY two actors – a man and a woman.

You are colleagues and also close friends. You have both applied for the same job which is a promotion. You have had your interviews and now you are waiting for the result. The secretary calls the woman back into the office and she is offered the job.

Scene:
In the waiting room – the woman returns and tells her friend and colleague that she has got the job. He wanted the job very badly – he can't help showing his envy and resentment. The man and the woman talk about what has happened.

The situation is then reversed and the man is offered the job.

The two actors then improvise the scene with the director giving them instructions. The group then script the play and rehearse it and at a later stage the play is performed for the class.

The class then discuss the play and decide whether the theme of 'Envy' is successfully conveyed.

Envy
Scene 1

Place: a waiting-room in a college. A man and a woman sit side by side in silence.

SECRETARY: [*enters*] So sorry to have kept you both waiting so long. Sue, could you come back in please.
[*She follows the secretary without looking back. He sits bolt upright – mouth open, expressing extreme surprise.*]
[*After a few minutes Sue returns, shyly at first.*]

SUE: [*quietly*] I got it, Jim. [*Talking to herself but getting louder and laughing.*] I can't believe it. I got the job. They chose me. Me.
[*Jim is slumped in his chair and turns to glare at her.*]

SUE: What's the matter? You don't mind do you?

JIM: [*mockingly*] Oh, no, no, not at all. I'm thrilled to pieces – couldn't be more pleased.

SUE: It hurts doesn't it?

JIM: Yes, it hurts.

SUE: It really does, doesn't it?

JIM: Grovel, grovel. [*Goes down on his knees.*] God, it hurts, yes, it bloody hurts.

SUE: It's your male ego, isn't it?

JIM: You are so sensitive. My God, why don't you crow? [*Makes crowing noises.*]

SUE: That's what I feel like doing. [*Laughs.*] I feel really super.

JIM: Well, go and do it somewhere else please. I feel bloody awful.

SUE: One of us had to get it. I worked harder than you. I deserved the job – come on, you know I did.

JIM: That's not the point. I'm a man.

SUE: [*Laughs*] You can't bear it can you, losing to a woman?

JIM: No, I can't.

SUE: Because I'm going to be in a higher position than you.

JIM: Well, I'm not going to hang around here. I can tell you that.

SUE: Why not?

JIM: Because I'm not going to put up with the bloody humiliation, that's why.

SUE: You're not going to put up with the humiliation?

JIM: No, I'm not.

SUE: Well, what would have happened if you'd got the job? I would have had to put up with it.

137

JIM:	That would have been your choice.
SUE:	What are you going to do then?
JIM:	I'm going to move on.
SUE:	So that's it. Our friendship ends because I've got a senior job to you.
JIM:	It's up to you.
SUE:	You want me to turn it down?
JIM:	Either you want my friendship or you want the job.
SUE:	That's not fair.
JIM:	If I hadn't worn this purple shirt you gave me I'd have got it. What are you laughing at?
SUE:	Because it's not true. It had nothing to do with the way you are dressed.
JIM:	What has it to do with then? Why in God's name should they have chosen you over me? I've a good mind to take it to the union. Discrimination, that's what it is.
SUE:	Discrimination? Discrimination against whom?
JIM:	Men, of course, men. You've got to be a woman to get on nowadays.
SUE:	How ridiculous.
JIM:	Did you tell them you'd take the job?
SUE:	Yes, of course.
JIM:	And you won't change your mind?
SUE:	No.
JIM:	Well, that's it then isn't it. Don't consider yourself a friend of mine from now on. Goodbye.

Scene 2
Lights up exactly the same scene as before but the couple have changed seats

| SECRETARY: | [*enters*] So sorry to have kept you both waiting so long. Jim, could you come back in please?
[*He jumps up enthusiastically, gives thumbs-up sign to colleague as he follows secretary. She remains seated looking dejected – puts her head in her hands.*]
[*One minute later he re-enters looking jubilant. Tries to hug companion and pull her to her feet. She resists and sits rigidly. She turns her face away.*] |
JIM:	Give me a kiss, Sue. Oh, come on. One of us had to get it.
SUE:	Yes one of us had to get it but it should've been me.
JIM:	Oh, don't be ...
SUE:	It meant a lot to me, you know that.
JIM:	I know, but you've still got a good job in the department.

138

SUE:	And you've got a better one.
JIM:	Oh, Sue, don't begrudge me.
SUE:	I do. I deserved that job more than you did – you know that. I've worked much harder than you. I needed it.
JIM:	Don't spoil it for me. I'm excited now. Say 'congratulations Jim boy.'
SUE:	No.
JIM:	Come on, we're best friends. My getting the job is like you getting it.
SUE:	You are a pig, aren't you? You weren't interested in the job until you knew I was applying for it, were you? You just wanted one up on me.
JIM:	What do you mean. Are we in competition?
SUE:	No, we are not in competition. I wanted that job for myself, not just to prove that I could get a better job than you. That's the only reason you applied.
JIM:	Rubbish. Anyway I honestly didn't think they'd give it to me. I just applied for a laugh. You've got more experience, I know, but you can help me. I'll need a lot of help.
SUE:	My God, you've got a nerve.
JIM:	Oh, come on Sue, I haven't had much have I?
SUE:	Much more than I have.
JIM:	God, you're a poor loser. I've not seen this in you before.
SUE:	It's not that I'm a poor loser. It's just that I go on and on losing to you all the time. You always get what you want. It's so easy for you.
JIM:	Why is it easy for me?
SUE:	Because you're a man. They think that a man must be better than a woman. It's not fair. That was my job. You've stolen my job. I hate you. Get out of my sight. [*She starts to cry.*]

I hope you have found this handbook useful and stimulating. No two teachers teach in the same way, but I have tried to provide ideas and examples based on my teaching which you may want to adapt and use.

I would like to know which bits of the book you used and how you used them, which bits didn't work and which did. You can contact me care of the National Extension College.

Good Luck.

Bibliography

Act English, Peter Watcyn-Jones, Penguin
An English Pronouncing Dictionary, Daniel Jones
British Book of Tongue Twisters, Ken Parkin
Development Through Drama, Brian Way, Longman
Drama Guidelines, Cecily O'Neill *et al.,* Heinemann Educational
Drama in Language Teaching, Susan Holden, Longman
Drama Techniques in Language Learning, Alan Maley and Alan Duff, CUP
Gamesters' Handbook, Donna Brandes and Howard Phillips, Hutchinson
Get Up and Do It, J. Dixey and M. Rinvolucri, Longman
Imaginary Crime, Robert Clark and Jo McDonough, Pergamon
Speech at Work, Audrey M. Bullard and E. Dulce Lindsay
The Art of Speaking Made Simple, William R. Gondin and Edward W. Mammen
Variations on a Theme, Alan Maley and Alan Duff, CUP
Voice and the Actor, Cicely Berry, Harrap
Your Voice and How to Use It Successfully, Cicely Berry
100 + Ideas for Drama, Anna Scher and Charles Verrall, Heinemann Educational